CATHOLIC
PERSPECTIVES

The
Right
to
Die

by
William May
and
Richard Westley

THE THOMAS MORE PRESS
Chicago, Illinois

ISBN 0-88347-115-9

CATHOLIC
PERSPECTIVES

The
Right
to
Die

PART ONE

by
William May

Introduction: *On Specifying the Issue*

IN his inaugural encyclical, *Redemptor Hominis,* Pope John Paul II strongly emphasized the inherent dignity and sanctity of man, male and female, the being for whom the Word became flesh. An illuminating section of the encyclical dealt with the question, "What modern man is afraid of." In it Pope John Paul said that "the man of today seems ever to be under threat from what he produces, that is to say, from the result of the work of his hands and, even more so, of the work of his intellect and tendencies of his will." In saying this, he was not opposing technological advancement as such. Rather he was expressing something that many people today experience, namely, a fear that part of what man produces, indeed "precisely that part that contains a special share of his genius and initiative, can radically turn against himself . . . producing an understandable state of disquiet, of conscious or unconscious fear and of menace."[1]

The menace of a technological civilization is dramatically illustrated by medical developments. We live in a world where the marvelous achievements of medical science and technology, inspired by a desire to protect the life and health of human beings, have made it increasingly difficult to die. It now makes sense to ask whether the medical "treatment" being given to some

5

persons is really helping them live or whether it is simply prolonging their dying. As a consequence, many people today are legitimately alarmed by the prospect that they and their loved ones will be "treated to death" and not allowed the opportunity to die in peace, in the company of their family and friends.

This has created a climate in which proponents of euthanasia or mercy killing are able to promote their views on the meaning of life and death by appealing to such slogans as "the right to die" and "death with dignity."[2] At the very beginning of this part of the book, then, it is imperative to clarify these expressions and the meaning of such terms as *active* and *passive* euthanasia and to sketch initially the position that will be developed.

The expression "the right to die" is, unfortunately, very ambiguous. In one sense it can be taken to mean the right that a human person has to be protected from offensive and intrusive treatments while that person is in the process of dying. If it is understood in this way, the expression is, in my opinion, acceptable. However, I would prefer to include our right to refuse unwanted and offensive treatments under our right to life and liberty as an aspect of our personal inviolability. The expression can also be taken to mean that human persons have the right to choose death for themselves and the right to the means, including the cooperation of others, to realize this choice. This is the sense in which the advocates of mercy killing understand the expression. I shall argue that we do not have a "right to die" in this sense.

There is a similar ambiguity in speaking of "death with dignity." Euthanasiasts propose death with dignity in an effort to win support for their view that we can rightfully choose death for ourselves or others in order to protect human dignity. Their understanding of this expression, however, differs from the way in which others, who regard willful self-destruction and the killing of others, even for the noble purpose of protecting dignity, as morally repugnant. Since this particular expression has received considerable popular support, there must be some important truth to which it points and which ought not to be overlooked. In attempting to express it we can, perhaps, see the reasons why it is so differently understood by euthanasiasts and those who disagree with them.

I believe that it can be put this way. Dignity means worth or intrinsic value. It is something intimately associated with the worth of human persons. Dignity is not regarded by us as an achievement but as an endowment. It is something that one has which is very close to one's simply being what and who one is. To the dignity inherent in the human person corresponds an attitude of respect due to that person by others and by society. When people say that they want to die with dignity they mean that they want to be recognized, in their dying and perhaps particularly at this period of their lives, for what and who they are. They want to be treated with the dignity due to them as persons; they do not want to be treated as if they were things or objects. When the expression, "death with dignity," is understood in this way, we would all agree that human persons ought to have death with dignity.

But when the euthanasiasts use this expression, they want it to mean something more. They want it to mean that some persons would be better off dead. They want it to mean that killing, in certain instances, can be the kindest possible treatment, the treatment most in accord with the dignity of the human person. They want it to mean that death itself is something good, a friend, and that death is preferable to life. By linking death with dignity they give death an excellence by association that it does not have of itself. They thus beg the question, for they assume that death is a good preferable to life and that killing can be a kindly act required by respect for the dignity of the human person. We all want to die with dignity, but most of us do not want to die at all. The central question is how we are to care properly for the dying and honor their dignity. Euthanasiasts, in appealing to "death with dignity," assume that the proper way to do this at times is to kill the dying because they will be better off dead than alive.[3]

Today it is customary to speak of two broad kinds of euthanasia, which the signers of "A Plea for Beneficent Euthanasia" (including Daniel C. Maguire, a leading Roman Catholic advocate of mercy killing) describe as "a mode or act of inducing or permitting death painlessly as a relief from suffering."[4] These are *active* and *passive* euthanasia. Active euthanasia is understood to include positive actions whose purpose is to kill a dying (or even nondying) person for reasons of mercy. Active euthanasia is, thus, an act of commission. Now we can kill someone either by doing something to that person or by failing to take action that will preserve or protect that person's life. If your baby slips in the bathtub and is submerged beneath the water and you simply watch the baby drown, you have killed the infant just as surely as if you had throttled it. Euthanasia can be administered in this way, too, so that there is good reason for speaking of *passive* euthanasia. The Down's Syndrome baby who was left in a room to starve to death after its parents and the doctors at Johns Hopkins Hospital decided that it would be better off dead than alive and thus that it was not morally necessary to correct, by simple surgery, an intestinal disorder that kept it from digesting its food, was killed by "passive" euthanasia.

Many advocates of euthanasia, however, including the signers of "A Plea for Beneficent Euthanasia," attempt to win support for their position by their use of this expression. Under "passive" euthanasia they include the decision to allow someone to die rather than to begin or continue the use of "extraordinary life-prolonging techniques."[5] They deny that there is any meaningful moral difference between killing someone and allowing someone to die.[6] Many other people, however, and I am among them, believe that there is a very significant difference between killing a person and allowing a person to die his or her own death, and they believe that it is not only morally right but at times morally required by a proper respect for the dignity of the dying person to let that person die. I shall return to this key distinction later. Here I want simply to stress that there is such a reality as "passive" euthanasia or killing someone by "benign neglect." The Mongoloid child in Johns Hopkins Hospital illustrates this. But the reality of this sort of human choice and behavior differs profoundly from the choice to withhold or withdraw "extraordinary" treatments and thus "allow" a person to die.

Euthanasia, whether active or passive, is further classified as being either voluntary, nonvoluntary, or involuntary. Euthanasia is voluntary if and only if the person killed is competent and gives informed consent

9

to being killed and if the person who does the killing does so on the belief that this person will be better off dead than alive. Euthanasia is nonvoluntary if the person killed is not competent to give such consent and the agent administers death on the belief that the person, if competent, would consent to being killed. Euthanasia is involuntary if the person killed is either competent to give consent and does not do so or, if incompetent, is assumed by the agent of death to be unwilling to consent were he able to do so.

None of the advocates of mercy killing in the United States today has as yet recommended involuntary euthanasia. Most, in fact, speak most frequently of voluntary euthanasia. Nonetheless it is clear, from the examples that are used, that they believe that nonvoluntary euthanasia is both morally right and ought to be legally permissible, particularly in coping with the difficulties presented by "defective" infants and some noncompetent senior citizens.[7]

With these preliminary observations on terminology in mind I now propose to examine the issues of euthanasia and the "right to die" in more detail. First I shall present the central arguments advanced by advocates of mercy killing, principally in an effort to disclose the major principles to which they appeal and the presuppositions underlying their arguments. Then I shall seek to offer a critique of their views. Finally, I shall present an alternative understanding of the meaning of life and death and of making good moral choices throughout life, even in its dying moments, and in caring for our dying siblings.

The Case for Killing Beneficently

THE case for euthanasia has been made by many writers.[8] Although there are differences, at times considerable, between, for example, a Joseph Fletcher and a Daniel Maguire,[9] all who defend euthanasia as morally right and advocate it as good public policy agree that we can "morally justify taking it into our own hands to hasten death for ourselves (suicide) or for others (mercy killing)."[10] They all affirm that at times it is "morally right and reasonable to terminate life through either positive action or calculated benign neglect."[11] They all judge that there are some persons who would be better off dead than alive and that it would be an act of kindness to kill them. I shall now summarize briefly the basic argument advanced to justify voluntary and nonvoluntary euthanasia and then attempt to show, by referring to the writings of some of the more prominent advocates of euthanasia, the presuppositions underlying this argument.

The basic argument for *voluntary euthanasia* can be fairly summarized as follows: In voluntary euthanasia the person to be killed kindly wishes to be killed; hence, no one is doing that person an injustice by killing him. The person's desire to be killed is reasonable in view of the suffering and/or humiliation he is experiencing; at times, others are suffering terribly too, psychologically or economically or both. Killing this person, who, after all, willingly consents to being killed and may even beg to be killed, is thus a reasonable way to end all this suffering. It is true that there are some persons in our society who object to killing of this kind on the grounds that it is immoral and constitutes an attack on some presumed "sanctity of life." Nonetheless, it would be both cruel and unjust to impose *their* values on someone who freely chooses to be killed and on those who seek compassionately to help this person realize this choice. Voluntary euthanasia is, therefore, morally right and ought to be legally permissible.[12]

In *nonvoluntary euthanasia* the individuals to be killed with kindness are by hypothesis incapable of consenting on their own behalf to being killed. Still, the argument goes, it is reasonable to believe that there are some conditions in which a quick and painless death is preferable to continuing a life that has lost value and meaning or that perhaps has never achieved value and meaning. Killing, it is urged, is a benefit rather than a harm, because life in some conditions is a burden and harmful and not a value. No one is treated unjustly if something harmful is taken away. Thus choosing to kill someone whose life is no longer a value to be preserved but is rather a burden to be carried, is a morally good choice and one that ought to be sanctioned by law.[13]

Although advocates of nonvoluntary euthanasia may themselves disagree over the precise criteria for determining when the conditions exist under which life is a burden and not a good, they concur with the view of Glanville Williams that "an assertion of the value of human life in the absence of all the activities that give meaning to life, and in the face of the disintegration of personality that so often follows from prolonged agony, will not stand scrutiny."[14] Some propose that in certain instances, for example, in the intensive care newborn nursery, we are confronted by individuals who are not persons although they are biologically members of the human species. Choosing to kill such nonpersons, therefore, raises no moral problems different in kind from those raised in choosing to kill other nonpersonal forms of life.[15]

These, basically, are the arguments advanced to support voluntary and nonvoluntary euthanasia, to defend the "right to die" in the sense that one has the right to be killed and "death with dignity" in the sense that we have the right to kill some persons as a way of showing respect for their dignity.

It is necessary now to turn to an examination of the presuppositions underlying these arguments. These presuppositions are implicit and are brought out more explicitly in the writings of the proponents of mercy killing. In a perceptive essay, Harvard University Professor Arthur Dyck suggested that four principal assumptions are at the heart of the ethics of euthanasia.[16] I believe that the four assumptions noted by Dyck (and set forth in note 16) can be summarized under the heading of an anthropological assumption, that is, an assumption concerning the meaning of being a human person. To this anthropological assumption can be joined a methodological one, that is, one concerned with the proper way to go about making good moral judgments. Each of these will now be described as they are found in the writings of some of the more prominent advocates of euthanasia.

13

The anthropological assumption holds that there is a sharp distinction to be made between *bodily* or *biological life* and *personal life;* the former is a condition for the latter and is of value only as the necessary substratum for the latter. Once the qualities associated with personal life are unrealizable, or until these qualities are attainable, bodily or biological life is of no real value. This assumption is central to the argument for nonvoluntary euthanasia and is easily discernible in it, whereas it is more implicit in the argument for voluntary euthanasia.

Perhaps the matter can be put this way. For those who advocate euthanasia, self-consciousness is the distinctive characteristic of humankind. The *person* is the self-conscious subject, aware of itself as a self and capable of controlling subpersonal nature, including bodily and physical life.

This understanding of the relationship between personal life and bodily life is reflected in the writings of the principal advocates of euthanasia. Here I shall examine briefly the writings of three such proponents, Joseph Fletcher, Daniel C. Maguire, and Marvin Kohl, insofar as their expression of this mentality is typical.

Fletcher is by far the most explicit in his presentation of this understanding of the person. This Episcopalian clergyman, who has for a long time championed the right to kill oneself and others for compassionate reasons and as a way of protecting human dignity, insists on the "right of spiritual beings to use intelligent control over physical nature rather than to submit beastlike to its blind workings."[17] He likens the morality of euthanasia to that of contraception, for he writes: "Death control, like birth control, is a matter of human dignity.

Without it persons become puppets."[18] Eloquently, he elaborates the right of persons to exercise dominion over physical nature, including bodily life and its processes, proclaiming:

> Physical nature—the body and its members, our organs and their functions—all of these *things* are a part of "what is over against us," and if we live by the rules and conditions set in physiology or another *it* we are not *thou*. . . . Freedom, knowledge, choice, responsibility—all these things of personal or moral value are in us, not *out there*. Physical nature is what is over against us, out there. It represents the world of *its*.[19]

Physical life, thus, for Fletcher, pertains to an impersonal world of nature, of "its." Man—that is, personal, conscious, rational man—has the right to dispose of this physical, impersonal "it" in order to serve such personal goods as freedom, choice, and responsibility.

Daniel C. Maguire, the most ardent Roman Catholic champion of "death by choice,"[20] is in substantive agreement with Fletcher that the human person—the conscious, rational subject—has the right to subject physical nature to rational control, and in the world of physical nature he includes the bodily life of the human person or what he terms "biochemical and organic factors." Echoing Fletcher, he proclaims that just as "birth control, for a very long time, was impeded by the physicalistic ethic that left moral man at the mercy of his biology" until "technological man discovered that he was morally free to intervene creatively and to achieve birth control by choice," so the same physicalistic ethic has condemned man "to await the good pleasure of biochemical and organic factors and allow these to determine the time and manner of his demise." Now, however, Maguire continues, technological man can creatively intervene, and has a moral right so to intervene, in order "to terminate life through either positive action or calculated benign neglect rather than to await in awe the dispositions of organic tissue."[21] Bodily life for Maguire is, as it is for Fletcher, a "merely biological" good, not a personal good.[22]

Marvin Kohl, the humanist philosopher who has argued extensively for euthanasia, emphasizes throughout his writings the supremacy of such human and personal values as dignity and rational control in comparison to the value of physical existence. Kohl acknowledges that many persons who oppose euthanasia do so on the grounds that it is destructive, not protective, of human dignity insofar as it is destructive of human life. He is willing to concede that one may legitimately speak of the inherent dignity of human beings as connoting "excellences that set human beings apart from other species,"[23] but he argues that this sort of dignity is not pertinent to the issue. What is of supreme importance is another sort of dignity, one that consists "in having reasonable control over the major and significant aspects of one's life."[24] This sort of dignity is for him the basis of our right to determine ourselves, and its exercise can at times require the choice to kill oneself or another. The central dignity of the person is "the actual ability of a human being to rationally determine and control his way of life and death and to have this acknowledged and respected by others."[25] It follows from this that bodily life as such is subordinate and inferior to personal dignity. Thus actions destructive of bodily life are morally justifiable and legally permissible if they can serve to enhance or protect the value of rational determination and control.

The views of these leading advocates of beneficent euthanasia are representative and enable us to understand the underlying concept of the human person and of the relationship of the person to bodily life in the arguments used to support both voluntary and nonvoluntary euthanasia. Since this notion of the human person undergirds the rationale for euthanasia, we ought not to be surprised that those who share it are inclined to refer to persons in comatose states, such as Karen Ann Quinlan, as "living vegetables," and to regard unborn children and the newborn children in intensive care nurseries as living members of the human species, biologically alive, but nonetheless not yet "persons."[26] Those who share this view are also inclined to want to redefine death in terms of the death of the cells of the neocortex of the brain, that part of the brain that is involved in rational thought.[27]

It is not to my purpose here to comment on this anthropological assumption underlying the arguments for "death by choice." Comments on it will be provided in a subsequent section of the essay. I want now to examine the other, methodological, assumption at the heart of the arguments for euthanasia.

The advocates of euthanasia adopt what can be called a *consequentialist* methodology in ethics.[28] By this I mean that they believe that the proper way to arrive at a good moral judgment, particularly in problematic or conflict situations such as those that confront us when we are trying to determine how we ought properly to care for a dying person, is to assess the consequences of

17

the various alternatives and then choose that alternative that promises to bring about the greatest good or at least to minimize evil. They admit that death, in some sense at least, is an evil, because, after all, most of us do not want to die. But they argue that the choice of death and the choice to kill are morally upright when ordered to the protection of a good that is greater than physical life itself, a good such as personal dignity. Death is a disvalue, an evil of sorts, but we can choose death as a means to a greater good.

This consequentialist methodology is articulated quite clearly by Joseph Fletcher and Daniel Maguire. Fletcher stresses that the end justifies the means. In saying this he does not mean that *any* end can justify *any* means; rather, he means that we may rightfully choose to do evil or to effect a disvalue if there is a proportionate good that will be served by doing so, a good that serves as a sufficient reason for the choice of evil. He thus writes: "The priority of the end is paired with the principle of 'proportionate good'; any disvalue in the means must be outweighed by the value gained in the end."[29] In some of his writings on questions other than euthanasia (for instance in his defense of dropping the atomic bombs on Nagasaki and Hiroshima and in his theoretical defense of genocide),[30] Fletcher determines the goodness of the end that can serve as a proportionate reason for choosing evil by a utilitarian calculus, that is, by simply counting the number of people who will be helped and those who will be hurt as a result of the action and then choosing the deed that will benefit most. But in the context of choosing death for oneself or another, the proportionate good that serves as the end and justifies the act of killing entailed is the good of personal integrity or human dignity.[31]

Maguire similarly presents a consequentialistic ethic, or an ethic of the proportionate good.[32] He argues that the most important thing to consider in determining whether it is morally right to choose to do an evil is "whether there is a proportionate reason to permit or intend [an evil such as death]."[33] This means that one can morally choose to do a deed that directly causes evil that the agent cannot not intend or will so long as there is a "proportionate reason" for doing so. A greater proportionate reason may be required if one is rightfully to intend the evil directly than if one merely permits or allows the evil to occur,[34] but the "basic category" for determining whether the deed is morally right is the category of proportionate reason.[35]

Applying this principle to the choice to kill oneself or another for reasons of mercy, Maguire holds that such deeds are morally right so long as a good greater than that of physical life is served, a good such as personal integrity or the freedom of self-determination. In other words, there is a weighing of values or goods, and the good of physical life is judged of lesser value than that of personal integrity or dignity. Hence the choice to destroy life for a set purpose can be a morally good choice, justified by the principle of proportionate reason or good.[36]

Since the arguments for mercy killing and the presuppositions undergirding these arguments have now been reviewed, it is opportune to offer some critical observations concerning them.

A Critique of the Ethics of Euthanasia

BEFORE presenting a critique of the presuppositions underlying the arguments for euthanasia, it will be of value to present some cogent counterarguments to them. It needs to be kept in mind that those who regard voluntary and nonvoluntary euthanasia to be morally upright modes of behavior logically want to see them legally accepted and adopted as social policy. For this to occur it will at least be necessary to change the laws concerning homicide. With respect to voluntary euthanasia there would be the need to establish some kinds of legal procedures, perhaps entailing governmental regulation, to make sure that persons who freely choose to be killed are in fact killed beneficently and that those who do not consent to being killed are not. Nonvoluntary euthanasia would require the establishment of criteria for determining when in fact physical life is no longer a boon but a burden.

As Yale Kamisar and many others have noted (most recently Germain G. Grisez and Joseph M. Boyle, Jr., in a painstaking and exhaustive study),[37] the legalization of voluntary euthanasia will inevitably work to the serious disadvantage of many persons who do not want to be killed. Once it is morally and legally permissible for a person to consent to being killed and for others to help accomplish this choice of death, many who do not

20

want to be killed will be under heavy pressure to give their consent to this "option." As Grisez and Boyle observe, "many who are mortally ill worry that they are a burden to others, feel guilty for the care they need, apologize when they must ask for some service."[38] Most of us have had the experience of seeking to comfort persons we love while they are dying, assuring them that ministering to their needs is not an unwanted imposition and even pleading with them to make their wants known. Once dying persons realize that they can, by availing themselves of the most technically efficient and "beneficent" solution to the problems they cause by persisting in living, relieve others of the burden of caring for them they will begin to suffer terrible feelings of guilt should they stubbornly and perhaps selfishly refuse to consent to being killed. We can be sure, too, that there will be numerous occasions when relatives, health-care personnel, social workers, and many others will urge the dying to consent to this merciful and kindly treatment. We can likewise be confident, as Grisez and Boyle note, that "health-care personnel and social workers who personally accept euthanasia are likely to treat those who persist in dying naturally with about as much respect as nonbelievers now tend to treat those Jehovah's Witnesses who desire health care but refuse blood transfusions."[39]

There are many other serious disadvantages that will result from the acceptance of voluntary euthanasia, many of them focusing on the abandonment of care of the suffering dying and on the cessation of the work now being done to learn more about relieving their suffering and meeting their needs.[40] The most compelling argument, however, against voluntary euthanasia is that it will inevitably cause injustices to many who do not wish to be killed and will seriously violate the liberty of all in our society who do not accept the worldview of the proponents of euthanasia. It has already been noted that the public acceptance of voluntary euthanasia will entail a change in laws concerning homicide and will require procedures to verify that only persons who want to be killed are so killed. The choice to be killed is, after all, a personal, private choice, one that does not foster a compelling public good. Should this choice be made legally available it will either demand extensive governmental regulation, no governmental regulation, or at least some measure of governmental regulation. Since this is so, I believe that the following argument, proposed by Grisez and Boyle, not only merits the serious consideration of every person but also provides a devastating refutation of the argument proposed to justify voluntary euthanasia. Grisez and Boyle argue as follows:

If voluntary euthanasia is legalized without regulation, those who do not wish to be killed are likely to become unwilling victims; this would deny them the protection they presently enjoy under the law of homicide. And since the denial is to serve a private interest, it will be an injustice. If voluntary active euthanasia is legalized with close regulation which will involve the government in killing, those who abhor such killing will be involved against their wishes, at least to the extent that their government and institutions will be utilized for this purpose. Since the government's involvement will be required only as a means to the promotion of a private interest, this state action will unjustly infringe the liberty of all who do not consent to mercy killing as a good to whose promotion state action might be legitimately directed. A solution involving a compromise between legalization of voluntary active euthanasia without regulation of the practice and legalization with close regulation which will involve the government in mercy killing would mean some degree of lessened protection together with some degree of governmental involvement—a situation which will result in injustice partly due to the reduced protection of the lives of those who do not wish to be killed and partly due to the unwilling involvement of those who do not wish to kill. Since the stated conditions are all the possible conditions under which voluntary active euthanasia could be legalized, legalization is impossible without injustice. Therefore, the legalization of voluntary active euthanasia must be excluded.[41]

This argument does not show that voluntary active euthanasia is morally wrong; still, it is in my opinion not only a cogent but an irrefutable argument against its legalization. If there are such strong reasons against the legalization of a form of behavior, there are good reasons to believe that it is not a morally sound practice, for morally good practices ought to be socially acceptable and legally permissible.

With respect to nonvoluntary euthanasia, or the beneficent killing of those incapable of giving consent to being killed because others judge that their lives are a burden and not a boon, the likelihood of causing serious injustice increases. After all, euthanasiasts themselves differ on the criteria that ought to be employed in determining when a particular life is no longer a value and can therefore be destroyed. There is a subjective arbitrariness involved here that is totally incapable of being governed by any intelligent principles. Here we ought to be able to learn from recent experience.

The practice of beneficent euthanasia as a way of caring for the lives of newborn "defective" children has been adopted in recent years and has been documented in an article, thoroughly sympathetic to the idea of nonvoluntary euthanasia and widely reported, by Drs. Raymond S. Duff and A. G. M. Campbell.[42] These doctors reported the deaths of 299 infants at Yale-New Haven Hospital over a thirty-month period from 1970-72. Of these, 256 died from existing pathological conditions despite the treatment given, but 43 of the infants died because of choices by parents and health care personnel not to provide treatment because their lives were judged not to be "meaningful" or because the infants were deemed not to be "lovable." No objective criteria, however, on which all could agree, were operative. What actually happened, as Paul Ramsey has so overwhelmingly demonstrated, is that arbitrary and subjective judgments about the meaningfulness of *others' lives* were substituted for objective judgments concerning the treatments that might be beneficial to them.[43] This would inevitably be the result were nonvoluntary euthanasia to become accepted. All this leads to is the imposition of someone else's judgment on the value of another someone's life.

The difficulty, indeed the absurdity, of seeking to determine when a particular human life is "meaningful" or not is poignantly illustrated by a famous New Jersey Supreme Court Case. The parents of a boy, Jeffrey Gleitman, who had been born congenitally defective in sight, hearing, and speech because his mother had contracted rubella in pregnancy, brought suit against the gynecologist-obstetrician, Cosgrove, on behalf of the boy on the grounds that he had suffered a "wrongful birth" and that his life was a burden, not a boon. The New

24

Jersey Supreme Court, in declaring against the Gleit-
mans, said:

> It is basic to the human condition to seek life and hold on
> to it however heavily burdened. If Jeffrey could have been
> asked as to whether his life should be snuffed out before
> his full term of gestation could run its course, our felt
> intuition of human nature tells us that he would most
> surely have chosen life with defects against no life at all.
> 'For the living there is hope, but for the dead there is
> none' (Thucydides). . . . The right to life is inalienable
> in our society. A court cannot say what defect should
> prevent an embryo from being allowed life. . . . A child
> need not be perfect to have a worthwhile life.[44]

Gleitman v. Cosgrove may be a case more germane
to the question of the abortion of unborn children who
are discovered to be suffering from maladies than it is
to the subject of nonvoluntary euthanasia of the already
born. Still, the judgment of the Court illumines the problems in establishing the criteria to determine objectively
when a human life is meaningful or not. Here it might
also be noted that the underlying presuppositions of the
ethics of euthanasia are the same as the presuppositions
underlying arguments for abortion. Although the practices are different, the principles in terms of which their
morality is to be judged are the same. It is thus no sur-
prise that those who defend abortion defend euthanasia,
nor is it surprising that the advocacy of the right to die,
in the sense of the right to be relieved of a meaningless
life, quickly follows efforts to make abortion legally permissible. Abortion of "defective" unborn children is
rightly called *fetal euthanasia*.

With these counterarguments to euthanasia in mind

we can now turn attention to the presuppositions upon which the arguments for euthanasia are based: the anthropological presupposition concerning the meaning of *person* and the relationship between the person and bodily life, and the methodological presupposition proposing a consequentialist weighing of values as the proper way to go about making good moral judgments and choices, particularly in problematic situations when no matter what we choose to do, some sort of evil will be experienced.

The anthropological presupposition of the ethics of euthanasia proposes that there is a sharp distinction to be made between *physical* or *bodily life* and *personal life*. On this presupposition there are two components of the human being. The one component, and the component that is something really good and valuable, is the personal. This personal component consists in the self-awareness of the human being, the human being's capacity to control affairs through personal choice, and the human being's capacity to enter into relationships with other selves. This personal component or "distinctively human" component of the human being is absent from some members of the human species, namely from those who, like the unborn and the newly born, have not as yet developed the capacity to be aware of themselves as selves and from those who, like the irreversibly comatose, have lost this capacity. The absence of this capacity is what makes such human beings to be likely candidates for nonvoluntary euthanasia (the difficulties arise in articulating the criteria for determining when this capacity is absent). It is the exercise of this capacity, which we could call the person-making capacity of a human being, that justifies the choice of those endowed with it to kill themselves or to ask to be killed, because this personal capacity is a good different from and superior to the nonpersonal bodily life of the human being. Bodily or biological life, which is nonpersonal in character, is the other component of the human being. This component, which is supposedly similar in nature to the life of vegetables and animals and in no way distinctively human, does exist in all living members of the human species, but its value is merely instrumental insofar as it serves as the necessary material condition for the existence of the distinctively human personal component.

This presupposition of the ethics of euthanasia is obviously a dualism of an extreme kind. It separates the human being into two elements, indeed two quite distinct entities, the one subhuman and subpersonal in character and the other personal and human. This dualism is, I submit, philosophically untenable and irreconcilable with Christian and Catholic faith. It is philosophically untenable because it conceives of the human being as a nonhuman plant (after all, the irreversibly comatose are referred to as "living vegetables") and a nonhuman animal (obviously, fetuses and newborn children are animals) to which is added a "person," and from which a "person" is taken away when the "person-making" capacities are lost. If this is the case, then a human being is not *one* entity, *one* being, but several: a vegetable, an animal, and a person, leading several lives. This view not only makes it impossible to understand how a human being can be *one* being, it renders utterly inexplicable our experienced unity of ourselves as ourselves. Our bodies are not tools or instruments that "we," personal subjects use, nor are they like clothes that we put on and take off. We personally *are* our bodies, and our bodies are our selves. As the philosopher Hans Jonas has put it:

> My identity is the identity of the whole organism, even if the higher functions of personhood are seated in the brain. How else could a man love a woman and not merely her brains? How else could we lose ourselves in the aspect of a face? Be touched by the delicacy of a frame? It's this person's, and no one else's. Therefore, the body of the comatose, so long as—even with the help of art—it still breathes, pulses, and functions otherwise, must still be considered a continuance of the subject that loved and was loved.[45]

The life of a living being is indistinguishable from the very reality of the being, a reality which pervades and includes everything that the being does. Biologically there is no question when a living member of the human species exists, and every living member of the human species is no plant or brute animal but a human being, living the life of a human being, and it is this life that permeates all activities of that human being, including such activities as thinking and choosing and loving. "Life," as Grisez and Boyle put it, "is not a characteristic of one part of a whole [the bodily aspect] and [personal] activities properties of some other part of it [the personal aspect]."[46] Rather the same life permeates all the activities of the one human being, the one human person. Thus when my *body* dies, *I* die. Death is not the separation of the "person" from the "body," it is the death of the whole person.[47]

A dualistic view of the human being makes a mockery of Christian and Catholic faith. When God created

Adam he did not create a living body to which he then added a "person," he created a living creature that was a person. When the Uncreated Word of God became flesh to share our humanity so that we could share his divinity, he did not take to himself a plant and animal nature to which some human epiphenomenon was added; he became a human being and took upon himself and incorporated into his person a fully human nature. When he was crucified on the cross, an animal body was not what was killed, but rather himself. In the Creed, when we speak of our hope in the resurrection of our very selves, we speak of the resurrection of the *body*.

The dualistic view of man central to the ethics of euthanasia may be compatible with a Stoic philosophy and understanding of human existence, for after all the Stoics heartily endorsed suicide and the right to be killed; it is not, I submit, intelligible for anyone who accepts the reality of living human flesh or for anyone who looks toward the resurrection of the body.

Bodily life is not merely a *condition for* human life, it is an integral *component of* human life, and human life is the life of a personal being, not a vegetable or animal being. Bodily life, therefore, participates in the dignity of a person.

Now let us examine the second, methodological, presupposition of the ethics of euthanasia. As will be recalled, this is the presupposition that the proper way to make good moral judgments and choices is to weigh alternative courses of action, balancing off their good and evil effects, and then choosing that alternative that will seemingly produce the greater balance of good over evil. It is the view that one can rightfully choose an evil, such as death, for the sake of some greater good, such as freedom and dignity. The consequentialist presupposes that we can "weigh" or "measure" the goods of human existence, goods such as life itself and health, freedom and dignity, justice and peace, knowledge and friendship. Of course, for the consequentialist who advocates euthanasia or the right to die in the sense of the right to be killed, *bodily* life will *always* be of less "weight" than such personal goods as liberty and dignity and friendship. Yet the general principle of consequentialist thinking is that we ought always to choose to do the deed that will bring about the greater or "greatest" good.

Now each of us would obviously agree with the view that one ought to choose that alternative that promises the greater good if by *good* is understood what is *morally* good, for the morally good choice is, after all, the one we are seeking to make in our efforts to shape our lives responsibly. But when the consequentialist proposes this as the fundamental principle for making moral choices he is not using the term *good* in a moral sense. He is referring to *good* in the sense that it designates some perfection or set of perfections that contribute to the flourishing of human persons and communities, to *good* in the sense that life and health, liberty and justice, human dignity and friendship, knowledge and peace, are "good." The consequentialist's assumption is that we can weigh or measure these goods in such a way that we can determine which among them is greater so that pursuing it is justifiable even if its pursuit requires us deliberately and of set purpose to destroy other goods.[48] In the debates over the "right to die," the euthanasiast-consequentialist assumes that it is morally right to choose death and to turn against life because doing so in some way serves such higher goods as dignity and freedom.

The difficulty with this view is that the basic goods of the human person are not measurable quantities that can be compared and balanced off against each other. They refer to different dimensions of our being and are simply not capable of being quantified and measured. How, for example, is it possible to compare the good of knowledge pursued for its own sake with the good of being treated justly or of being in a state of good health or of being alive? The fact is that all of these are goods of human persons and contribute to human flourishing. Human beings commit themselves to the pursuit of these goods, and their doing so is intelligent and appropriate. Those in the health-care professions commit themselves to the good of human life and health, whereas lawyers and others commit themselves to the good of justice, teachers and others to the good of knowledge. It would be arrogant for a doctor to claim that the good he chooses to pursue is measurably superior to the good of justice pursued by lawyers or the good of knowledge pursued by scholars. Yet for consequentialism to be true, there must be some way to measure the goods that go to make up the whole human good, to compare them in such a way that one can clearly determine, in situations when various goods appeal to us in different ways, which is the "better" or "higher." The attempt to do so is doomed to failure, and this accounts for the reasons why different consequentialists differ sharply among themselves in determining the "greater" good. Because the goods of the human person are in truth incomparable (and it may be suggested that they are

31

so because the human person is of incomparable worth
and the goods contributing intrinsically to the flourishing of the human person participate in the incomparable
worth of the person), there is no clearly unambiguous
way to weigh and balance them off against each other.
Thus consequentialists end up by arbitrarily asserting
that one or another is measurably greater than another.[49]

Other objections can be raised against consequentialism as a method for making moral judgments and
choices[50] in addition to the fact that it is predicated upon
an attempt to measure the incommensurable and compare the incomparable. One that in my view is telling
is the fact that consequentialism is a form of extrinsic-
ism. By this I mean that it determines the rightness or
wrongness of human acts, such as the act of killing a
person, by factors extrinsic to the acts themselves,
namely by their consequences or effects.[51] The consequentialist seeks to determine whether a proposed course
of human action is right or wrong by attempting to discover what that act will achieve or get done. But as
many authors, particularly Herbert McCabe, note, our
acts not only *get something done,* they *get something
said.*[52] They have something to tell us about ourselves
and the kind of persons we are. They are, in other
words, intelligible, and we can discover their meaning
and intelligibility. By our willingness to do the deeds
we do, we take on, as part of our moral identity, the
identity of doers of certain sorts of deeds. Thus if we
are willing to do what is in truth an act of killing a
fellow human person, we take on, as part of our moral
identity, the identity of killer, even if we seek to conceal
or hide this identity from ourselves. And, I submit, we
ought not to be willing to take on the identity of killers,

for in giving to ourselves this kind of identity we are failing to become the beings that we are meant to be.[53]

The consequentialist, by identifying the moral meaning of our acts with their results or consequences, is really engaging in a form of deception. The consequentialist succumbs to the temptation to *redescribe* a human act in terms of its intended consequences and in doing so ignores or hides from view the very meaning of the act.[54] Thus the consequentialist redescribes the act of starving a crippled newborn to death as an act of "kindness" or of giving a lethal drug to a cancer victim as an act of "mercy." We all want to be kind and merciful, for these are desirable human traits, but the consequentialist begs the question by redescribing as kind an act that may in fact not be a kindly deed but rather a deadly deed, a deed destructive of a truly human good, the good of life.

The ethics of euthanasia has now been described and criticized. It is now necessary to propose an alternative, one that respects the right of human persons to be cared for with dignity in their dying, one that affirms the right of dying human persons to be protected from intrusive and offensive treatments and to be given the companionship of family and friends, and one that honors their lives by refusing to kill them.

An Alternative to Euthanasia:
An Ethics of Dying Well

SINCE the presuppositions undergirding the ethics of euthanasia were examined and criticized in the previous section, it seems advisable to begin this section on an ethics of dying well[55] by setting forth its anthropological and methodological presuppositions.

Its first or anthropological presupposition is that the body and bodily life are intrinsic, substantive goods of the human person and not material and subpersonal conditions for personal existence. It regards life as a good *of* the person, not a good *for* the person. Indeed, for the Catholic Christian, life itself is seen as a good gift from God, a precious, irreplaceable, and incomparable good participating in the goodness of God himself and in the goodness of the human beings who are his created words and images. Life is by no means the highest good or the *summum bonum;* it is not an absolute good in this sense, nor are any other truly human goods, such as the good of dignity or the good of freedom, absolute in this sense, for only God is the highest good, the *summum bonum,* the absolute good. But life, like dignity and freedom, is a good, not an evil; it is a blessing, not a curse; and as such it should elicit from the human heart a response of gratitude and awe-filled thanksgiving.[56] The ethics of dying well conceives of the human person as living human flesh, as flesh similar to

34

the living flesh of animals but as flesh that is uniquely different in kind because it is the flesh of the human person.[57]

The second or methodological presupposition of the ethics of dying well is nonconsequentialist in character. This nonconsequentialist ethics is rooted in the thought of Thomas Aquinas and in the whole Judeo-Christian tradition. It agrees with St. Paul that we ought not freely choose to do evil so that good may come about (Romans 3.8), and it therefore rejects the view, central to consequentialist thought and to the ethics of euthanasia, that a good end can justify the doing of evil.

On this view, as Arthur Dyck and Paul Ramsey have fittingly observed, a person "does not choose death but how to live while dying."[58] As Ramsey continues, " 'choosing how to live while dying' stands in diametrical opposition to actions that 'have the immediate intention of ending life (one's own or another's).' Only the latter 'repudiates the meaningfulness and worth of one's own life.' Only the latter 'irrevocably severs any actual or potential contact with others and shuts them out of one's life.' Only the latter usurps dominion, claims co-regency, or throws back the gift in the face of the giver. Only the latter chooses death as means or end. The former is a life-choice, one among the choices of a life still received."[59]

This nonconsequentialist ethics begins with the principle that *good is to be done and pursued and evil is to be avoided.*[60] This principle is accepted as a truth needing no demonstration and incapable of being demonstrated, for its truth is evident once one understands what is meant by *good* and by *evil. Good* means what is truly perfective of a being, what any being needs if that being is to be what it is meant to be, and *evil* means the deprivation of good. This principle is the starting point or beginning of all intelligent human activity. No matter what any one of us does, whether it is morally right or morally wrong, we do it because we believe that by doing so we are achieving something good. No one chooses evil for the sake of evil. We may choose what we know to be morally wicked or evil, but even in choices of this sort we are seeking some good, and we attempt to justify or rationalize our choices both to ourselves and to others by appealing to some good that we hope to achieve through the act we choose to do.[61]

The human good, as we have seen, is pluriform. There are many goods of the human person, each contributing in its own unique way to the flourishing of human persons and human communities. Among these are the goods of life and health, freedom and dignity, friendship and peace.[62] As such these goods are nonmoral, for after all, a person is not a wicked person because he or she lacks friends or is sick or is treated ignominiously. Still, these goods are real goods of human persons and as such are worthy of human choice; we need these goods if we are to be fully ourselves, and we have a right to participate in these goods.[63] The evils destructive of them are the evils we are to avoid in our choices.

Moral considerations arise when we relate these goods to the human will or, to speak biblically, to the human heart. The person whose heart is open to God—the morally upright person—is the one who is open to these real goods of human persons and to their realization, both in himself *and* in others. None of these goods is, as we have seen, the highest good or "absolute" good in the sense of being the be-all and end-all of human existence, for only God is the highest good or *summum bonum*. But a human person freely determines his or her moral identity, his or her moral being, by his or her attitude toward these real goods of human persons and toward the persons in whom they are realized. Since these goods are truly goods of the human person, we ought to be ready to acknowledge them as such. They specify the sorts or kinds of good that we are to do and pursue, and the evils depriving us and others of them are the evils that we are to avoid in our action.[64] Each of these goods, and life itself is among them, is really worthy of human choice because each is a good *of* persons, not a good *for* persons. Since none of these basic human goods is the absolute good, the be-all and end-all of our existence, none ought to be regarded as such and made to function as the key to solving difficult situations; none, in short, is the measurably "greater" or "greatest" good postulated by consequentialism for whose sake we are to be willing deliberately and of set purpose to destroy other goods of the human person, to close our hearts to their goodness. With respect to the questions with which we are concerned, this means that "dignity" and "liberty" are not measurably superior goods for whose sake we may deliberately and of set purpose repudiate the good of life.

In other words, because each of these goods is really something good and hence worthy of human choice and love, we ought to be *unwilling* to set our wills, our hearts, our persons, against any one of them and to say, effectively through our actions, that any one of them is here and now not a good but an evil. This means that we ought to be unwilling to choose, deliberately and of set purpose, acts in which we propose to destroy any of these goods for the sake of some other human good; we ought to be unwilling to do evil so that good may come about. It is for this reason that this nonconsequentialistic ethics believes that it is morally wrong to kill, to close one's heart to the good of human life.

We may rightly choose to do an act that is itself targeted on the protection of a basic human good when this is being imperiled, even if the act will foreseeably lead to the loss of some other human good, when there are no other alternatives for protecting the imperiled good and there are no morally compelling reasons for us to refrain from acting.

In the previous paragraph I have tried to summarize the thinking behind the celebrated "principle of double effect." This principle, which Paul Ramsey believes is rooted in Christian love as well as in the natural law,[65] has had a long history. Foreshadowed in St. Augustine and in its essential features integrated by St. Thomas into his moral thought,[66] this principle is particularly significant in regard to actions destructive of human life. Because human life is a good that requires our love and respect, we ought not to choose to do deeds that are, in truth, deeds of killing; we ought not to take on ourselves the identity of *killers*. Yet there are times when we may rightfully choose to do a deed that is itself protective of a human life that is being threatened, even if we foresee that by doing so another human life will, tragically, be lost. In such instances, if there are no other alternatives and if there are no compelling moral reasons to refrain from acting, *our* intent and the intent of our act is to protect and save a life that is threatened, not to take a life.[67] The euthanasiast, however, proposes precisely to do a deed whose precise purpose is to destroy a life, not save a life.

The basic presuppositions of the ethics of dying well have now been presented. This ethics instructs us, as does God himself, to choose life, not death. A human being ought not directly and of deliberate intent take human life, either his own or another's, not only because human life is itself a real human good, a created participation in the goodness of God himself and a good gift from him, but also because our existence together as human persons requires us to respect the life that lives in each one of our fellow human beings. Life is a gift that we receive ultimately from God, but proximately we receive it from our human persons, from our parents and from those with whom we live and move and have our being. We hold our lives at the leave of and mercy of our fellows, and the deliberate choice to repudiate human life is destructive not only of the covenant that God wills to exist between himself and us, but the covenant that he wills to exist in and among mankind.

Yet in this ethics life itself is not the only good of human persons; it is not the absolute good, the *summum bonum*. The ethics of dying well is not, as some euthanasiasts claim,[68] a *vitalistic* ethic, erecting life itself into the highest good. The ethics of dying well values *all* human goods, including life, dignity, and liberty, but it recognizes that God, and God alone, is the highest good or *summum bonum*. It holds that a human person's *moral* good is constituted by that person's willingness to love all true goods of human persons as they ought to be loved and to love God above all created human goods. Created human goods such as life and liberty and dignity are to be loved and ought never to be repudiated of set purpose, but they are not to be loved as the be-all and end-all of human existence.

Thus human life is not a good that is to be clung to no matter what. If clinging to it, or attempting to preserve it, requires us to *turn against* other human goods, such as dignity or freedom or integrity or justice, such actions of preserving life are wicked and immoral. Although death is *not* a good and is *not* worthy of human choice and love, neither is it an evil that is to be prevented at all costs. It is an event that closes our mortal existence, a reality that we must accept and experience and can never avoid. A human person has the right to refuse treatments that needlessly prolong the dying process and, in doing so, attack the goods of liberty and dignity.

The ethics of dying well teaches us that a human person does have the right to accept, in a humanly free and dignified way, his or her own death. It is for this reason that this ethics holds that we are not only morally free to allow or permit both ourselves and others to die but also that we are at times morally obliged to do so. The ethics of dying well takes seriously the distinction between killing, whether actively or passively by benign neglect, and allowing death to occur. This distinction, which the euthanasiasts scorn or seek to caricature, is valid. Human choice and action are involved both in killing by omission and in allowing death, but there is a moral chasm between these two sorts of choices and actions. When someone is killed by someone else's omitting an action, by "benign" neglect, the purpose of the omission is to bring death about; the purpose is to kill. The cause of death is the failure to do what can be and ought to be done to prevent death.

When a person is allowed to die, there is no choice of death by either active commission or passive omission. The person dies not because a requisite action has been omitted but because of an underlying disease or injury. Nothing is done with the intent of killing; rather treatment is withheld or withdrawn because it is no longer of medical benefit to the dying person and is in fact destructive of other human goods, such as liberty and dignity.[69]

Traditionally, medical ethics has distinguished between *ordinary* and *extraordinary* means of preserving life. The former have been regarded as mandatory or morally obligatory, so that to omit them is to choose death and to choose to kill by "benign neglect." The latter have been regarded as elective.[70] This distinction is a moral, not a medical distinction, so that the term "ordinary" ought not to be understood as standard medical practice or to refer to techniques that are commonly available, such as intravenous feedings or insulin injections, or, today, the use of respirators and other devices commonly found in hospitals. A procedure that may be ordinary in a medically technological sense may be extraordinary in the moral sense. The terms have a great deal of relativity, not because of any moral relativism, but because they are intended to direct attention to *objective* features in the patient's condition, features that differ from one person to another.

Today these terms are causing confusion. Paul Ramsey suggests that we discard this older language, which was intended to focus attention on objective conditions of the patient-person, and in its place substitute "medically indicated" and "medically nonindicated" treatments. A treatment is medically indicated when it will benefit the patient-person by adding life to his days and not simply by adding days to his life, whereas a treatment is not medically indicated when it would simply add days to one's life or, better, simply prolong one's dying.[71] I believe that one key way to determining whether a particular treatment is "ordinary" and thus "medically indicated" and morally obligatory, is to ask whether withholding or withdrawing it is equivalent to a proposal to kill the person. If it is, then the treatment is "ordinary" and morally mandated; if it is not, then it is a treatment that may be chosen or elected by a patient competent to choose for himself or herself, but it is not a treatment whose omission will kill by neglect.[72]

The ethics of dying well is an ethics that seeks to help people prepare for death and accept death, both those who are dying and those who are caring for the dying. As Elisabeth Kübler-Ross has shown, it takes time both for the dying person and for that person's loved ones to accept the fact of death, the harsh reality of this final indignity.[73] Killing the dying person robs both that person and that person's loved ones of the opportunity to prepare for death.

The ethics of dying well is an ethics that lies at the heart of the hospice movement. As Dr. Cicely Saunders and those who have worked closely with her have shown, true care for the dying incorporates compassion for suffering and respect for life. This care resolutely refuses to kill, for killing is neither kind nor caring.[74] Care reaches out to accompany another in that other's dying; it respects the other's right to be protected from unwanted, intrusive, nonmedically indicated treatments and it sees the life of that other, even in that other's dying, as a good worthy of human love and respect, as something meaningful.

The Roman Catholic Church teaches unequivocally that human life is a good and as such worthy of human choice and love. For this reason it teaches that "whatever is opposed to life itself, such as any type of murder, genocide, abortion, euthanasia, or willful self-destruction, . . . all these things are infamies indeed . . . and are a supreme dishonor to the Creator."[75] In the foregoing pages I have sought to offer reasons to support this teaching and to articulate an ethics that respects life and the right of human persons to life. This ethics teaches that our right to life includes the right to liberty and dignity; it honors our right to live while dying and to be treated with the dignity of human persons in dying. It likewise holds that all members of the human species, all living flesh of humankind, are equally precious and irreplaceable icons or images of the living God. It does not, as does the ethics of euthanasia, divide the human species into categories, deeming some members of the species as nonpersons or "vegetables," leading meaningless lives, and others (obviously including the advocates of death by choice, whether that choice be the active "termination of life," to use the euphemism employed, or its killing by "benign" neglect) as "persons" and therefore worthy of respect.

The ethics of euthanasia is well described as an ethics that advocates "death by choice." It is an ethics that chooses death, not life, and it is therefore an ethics that will lead to the destruction of life, and with the destruction of life it will lead also to the destruction of liberty and justice and all the other goods of human persons and communities. The ethics of dying well is an ethics of living well. It is an ethics that chooses life, not death; it is an ethics that respects the goods of liberty and justice and dignity and that will enable human persons and communities to flourish. It is an ethics that can give human beings the strength to cope with death and suffering, for it is an ethics that is rooted in a faith in God,[76] the best friend humankind has and one who has chosen to suffer death himself in the person of his Un-created Word-made-living-flesh precisely so that we may have life and have it more abundantly. I propose this ethics as one worthy of human persons and of human rights. The "right to die" ethics can give us only death.

Notes

1. Pope John Paul II, *Redemptor Hominis,* n. 15.

2. Some recent history is instructive here. Proponents of euthanasia had been seeking, with no success, both in England and in the United States, to secure passage of Voluntary Euthanasia Acts since 1936. By 1967, the Euthanasia Society of America (founded in 1938) realized that it was making little progress in achieving its goals. Its members thus decided to take a different route by speaking of the right to die and, at the suggestion of Dr. Luis Kutner, by advocating the "living will," not quite what they wanted but something in the neighborhood and, moreover, appealing to many who would vigorously resist the notion of mercy killing. At that time the Euthanasia Society was reorganized; it adopted a new name, the Society for the Right to Die, and established an affiliate, the Euthanasia Education Fund (later called the Euthanasia Educational Council), to serve as a tool for propaganda. In recent years the efforts of the Society for the Right to Die have, apparently, begun to pay off. Many "death with dignity" bills have been introduced in state legislatures and some have been passed. Although none so far is quite what the Euthanasia Society (=Society for the Right to Die) really wants, many are modeled after the Voluntary Euthanasia Bills introduced into the British Parliament since 1936 (and never passed). For more on this see Paul Marx, *Death Without Dignity* (Collegeville, Minn.: Liturgical Press, 1978) and Germain G. Grisez and Joseph M. Boyle, Jr., *Life and Death With Liberty and Justice: A Contribution to the Euthanasia Debate* (Notre Dame, Ind.: University of Notre Dame Press, 1979), pp. 251-259.

3. On this see Grisez and Boyle, *op. cit., pp.* 96-97, 174-175.

4. "A Plea for Beneficent Euthanasia," by Marvin Kohl and Paul Kurtz (signed by numerous theologians, philos-

ophers, and academics, including Maguire), in *Beneficent Euthanasia,* edited by Marvin Kohl (Buffalo, N.Y.: Prometheus Books, 1975), p. 234.

5. *Ibid.,* p. 235.

6. Thus Joseph Fletcher, "Ethics and Euthanasia," *American Journal of Nursing* 73 (April, 1973) 670-671; thus also James Rachels, "Active and Passive Euthanasia," *New England Journal of Medicine* 292 (January 9, 1975) 78-80.

7. Thus Daniel C. Maguire, after citing Millard S. Everett to the effect that "no child should be admitted into the society of the living" who suffers "any physical or mental defect that would prevent marriage or would make others tolerate his company only from a sense of mercy," offers no disagreement with such views. See his *Death by Choice* (New York: Doubleday, 1974; paperback ed. New York: Schocken Books, 1975), p. 7.

8. Principal writings of euthanasiasts include: Glanville Williams, *The Sanctity of Life and Criminal Law* (New York: Alfred C. Knopf, 1957); A. B. Downing, ed., *Euthanasia and the Right to Death* (London: Peter Owen, 1969) (among the contributors is Joseph Fletcher); Marvin Kohl, *The Morality of Killing: Sanctity of Life, Abortion and Euthanasia* (New York: Humanities Press, 1974); Kohl, ed. *Beneficent Euthanasia;* Maguire, *op. cit.;* Marya Mannes, *Last Rights* (New York: William Morrow and Co. 1974).

9. Maguire, in addition to *Death By Choice,* has two articles advocating mercy killing. One, "The Freedom to Die," was originally printed in *Commonweal,* August 11, 1972, and is reprinted in *New Theology #10,* edited by Martin E. Marty and Dean Peerman (New York: Macmillan, 1973); the other, "A Catholic View of Mercy Killing," is found in Kohl, *Beneficent Euthanasia,* pp. 34-43. In *Death By Choice,* p. 120, he recognizes, for instance, the legitimacy of the distinction between killing and allow-

ing to die. Nonetheless he thinks this distinction of little crucial moral significance. It is instructive to note that he was among the signers of "A Plea for Beneficent Euthanasia" (cf. notes 4 and 5), and it is evident that he must agree that omitting "extraordinary" treatment is "passive euthanasia." This is true, however, only if allowing to die is the same as killing by benign neglect.

10. Fletcher, "Ethics and Euthanasia," *loc. cit.,* 673.

11. Maguire, "The Freedom to Die," in *New Theology #10,* p. 189.

12. For this argument see the following: Arval Morris, "Voluntary Euthanasia," *Washington Law Review* 45 (1970) 251-254; *A Plan for Voluntary Euthanasia* (London: Euthanasia Society, 1962), pp. 5-9; Glanville Williams, *The Sanctity of Life and the Criminal Law,* pp. 311-329; Williams, "Mercy-Killing Legislation: A Rejoinder," *Minnesota Law Review* 43 (1958) 1-5; Marvin Kohl, "Understanding the Case for Beneficent Euthanasia," *Science, Medicine and Man* 1 (1973) 111-119.

13. On this see Williams, *The Sanctity of Life and the Criminal Law,* pp. 316-319; Kohl, *The Morality of Killing,* p. 96; Maguire, *Death by Choice,* pp. 23-26, 250, 173-177; Mannes, *op. cit.,* 92-99.

14. Williams, *The Sanctity of Life and the Criminal Law,* p. 316.

15. On this see Michael Tooley, "Abortion and Infanticide," *Philosophy and Public Affairs,* 3 (Fall, 1972) 37-65; H. Tristram Englehardt, "Ethical Issues in Aiding the Death of Young Children," in Kohl, ed., *Beneficent Euthanasia,* pp. 180-192. Here "aiding the death" is a euphemism for killing.

16. Arthur Dyck, "An Alternative to an Ethics of Euthanasia," in *To Live and To Die,* edited by Robert Williams (New York: Springer Verlag, 1972), pp. 98-112. On pp. 100-101 Dyck says that the presuppositions of the ethics of euthanasia are: (1) a human being's life is at the

disposal of that person to do with it as he or she wishes; (2) the dignity of the person by reason of his freedom of choice includes the freedom to kill oneself and to consent to being killed; (3) there comes a time when life has no worth either because of pain, suffering, or other distress; and (4) the supreme good is human dignity.

17. Fletcher, "The Patient's Right to Die," in Downing, *op. cit.,* p. 69.

18. *Ibid.*

19. Fletcher, *Morals and Medicine* (Boston: Beacon, 1960), p. 211.

20. For his principal writings on this subject see note 9. Maguire appeals, in support of his views, to the teaching of St. Thomas in *Summa Theologiae,* 1-2, 94, 4 and 5, to the effect that remote precepts of natural law bind "for the most part," but are defective in "some particular cases." Maguire abuses Aquinas. Aquinas definitely held that suicide is *always* wrong and that it is intrinsically evil to slay the innocent with direct intent, something Maguire himself knows full well. For a proper understanding of the Thomistic texts Maguire abuses see R. A. Armstrong, *Primary and Secondary Natural Law Precepts in Thomistic Natural Law Teaching* (The Hague: Martinus Nijhoff, 1966).

21. Maguire, "The Freedom to Die," *loc. cit.,* pp. 188-189.

22. It is for this reason that Maguire, like Fletcher, regards unborn children and infants as nonpersons, as entities perhaps on their way to personhood, but not as yet persons. See *Death by Choice,* ch. 9.

23. Kohl, "Voluntary Beneficent Euthanasia," in Kohl, *Beneficent Euthanasia,* pp. 132-133.

24. *Ibid.*

25. *Ibid.*

26. Thus Fletcher, "Indicators of Humanhood," *Hastings Center Report* 2 (November, 1972) 1-2 and "Four Indicators of Humanhood: The Enquiry Matures," *Hastings*

Center Report 4 (December 1974) 7, Tooley (cf. note 15), Englehardt (cf. note 15), and many others write.

27. On this see Grisez and Boyle, *op. cit.,* pp. 59-75 for a review of the literature.

28. Some writers, e.g. William Frankena in his influential *Ethics* (2nd ed.: Englewood-Cliffs, N.J.: Prentice-Hall, 1973), speak of teleological systems and deontological systems of ethics. Consequentialism is teleological in the sense in which Frankena uses this term. But so too are the various "mixed deontologies" of which he speaks and the "mediating approaches" of which Richard A. McCormick writes (cf. McCormick's "Genetic Medicine: Notes on the Moral Literature," *Theological Studies* 33 (September, 1972, 531), insofar as such approaches resolve problematic situations by seeking to do the deed that will bring about the "greatest" or "greater" good.

29. Fletcher, "Ethics and Euthanasia," *loc. cit.,* 674.

30. On this see Fletcher in *Hello, Lovers! An Invitation to Situation Ethics,* by Joseph Fletcher and Thomas Wassmer, edited by William E. May (New York: Corpus Books, 1970), p. 116.

31. This is clearly brought out in both "Ethics and Euthanasia," in "The Patient's Right to Die," in the Downing Symposium (cf. note 8), and in Fletcher's contribution to Kohl's *Beneficent Euthanasia,* "The 'Right' to Live and the 'Right' to Die," pp. 44-56.

32. I have previously criticized this in a number of places. See *Human Existence, Medicine, and Ethics* (Chicago: Franciscan Herald Press, 1977), pp. 59-65; see Germain G. Grisez, "Against Consequentialism," *American Journal of Jurisprudence* 33 (1978).

33. Maguire, "A Catholic View of Mercy Killing," in Kohl, *Beneficent Euthanasia,* pp. 39-40.

34. This point, accepted by Maguire (cf. *Death by Choice,* pp. 120-122) is developed by Richard A. McCormick in his *Ambiguity in Moral Choice* (Milwaukee: De-

partment of Theology, Marquette University, 1973), p. 77 ff.

35. Maguire, *Death by Choice,* pp. 126-127.

36. This is the basic argument developed by Maguire in *Death by Choice,* "The Freedom to Die," and "A Catholic View of Mercy Killing."

37. See Yale Kamisar, "Some Non-Religious Views Against Proposed 'Mercy Killing' Legislation," *Minnesota Law Review* 42 (1958) 970-1041; Grisez and Boyle, *op. cit.,* pp. 149-183.

38. Grisez and Boyle, *op. cit.,* p. 150.

39. *Ibid.,* p. 151.

40. *Ibid.,* p. 151.

41. *Ibid.,* pp. 153. See pp. 154-168 for an extended defense of the argument given.

42. Raymond S. Duff and A. G. M. Campbell, "Moral and Ethical Dilemmas in the Special-Care Nursery," *New England Journal of Medicine* 289, no. 17 (October 25, 1973) 885-894.

43. Paul Ramsey, *Ethics at the Edges of Life* (New Haven: Yale University Press, 1978), pp. 189-267.

44. *Gleitman v. Cosgrove,* 49 NJ 22, 227 A.2d 689 (1967) 693.

45. Hans Jonas, *Philosophical Essays: From Ancient Creed to Technological Man* (Englewood Cliffs, N.J.: Prentice-Hall, 1974), p. 139.

46. Grisez and Boyle, *op. cit.,* p. 377.

47. Here the words of St. Thomas in *Super primam epistolam ad Corinthos lectura,* XV, lec. ii, are pertinent: "man naturally desires the salvation of his very self. Now although the soul is a part of the body of man, it is not the whole man. My soul is not me. Hence although the soul might find salvation in another life, I would not, nor would any man whatsoever." Here I would like to note that I think we are, in one sense, *animals.* But we are, as René Dubos puts it, "so *human* an animal." We are radically *different in*

kind from other animals so that our animality differs radically from the animality of other animals.

48. Here I would note that the consequentialism followed by Maguire has been adopted by many contemporary Roman Catholic moralists. The leading advocate in this country of this view is Richard McCormick, S.J. In addition to *Ambiguity in Moral Choice* see his essay in *Doing Evil to Achieve Good,* edited by Richard A. McCormick and Paul Ramsey (Chicago: Loyola University Press, 1978). His basic argument is that it is morally right directly to intend evil, that is, the destruction of a real human good, if there is some proportionate good that will serve as a sufficient reason.

49. On this, see Paul Ramsey, "Incommensurability and Indeterminancy in Moral Choice," in *Doing Evil To Achieve Good,* pp. 69-144; Germain G. Grisez, "Against Consequentialism," *American Journal of Jurisprudence* 33 (1978).

50. One of the most telling, developed by Grisez in the article cited in note 49 and also by him and Boyle in *Life and Death With Liberty and Justice,* pp. 346-355, is that consequentialism destroys freedom of choice because it leads to psychological determinism.

51. On this see Eric D'Arcy, *Human Acts: An Essay in Their Moral Evaluation* (Oxford: Oxford University Press, 1965), pp. 1-40; Paul Ramsey, *Deeds and Rules in Christian Ethics* (New York: Charles Scribner's Sons, 1967), pp. 193-229; William E. May, "The Moral Meaning of Human Acts," *Homiletic and Pastoral Review* (October, 1978).

52. Herbert McCabe, *What Is Ethics All About?* (Washington: Corpus Books, 1969), pp. 91-92.

53. I seek to develop this idea in *Human Existence, Medicine, and Ethics,* Introduction.

54. On the consequentialist redescription of acts in terms of consequences, see D'Arcy, *op. cit.*

55. Arthur Dyck (cf. work cited in note 16) calls this

an ethics of *benemortasia;* Paul Ramsey, in *Patient As Person* (New Haven: Yale University Press, 1971), pp. 113-164, uses the term *agathanasia.*

56. Ramsey develops this thought beautifully in *Ethics at the Edges of Life,* pp. 207-208.

57. On our difference from other animals, see Mortimer Adler, *The Difference of Man and the Difference It Makes* (New York: Meridian, 1968).

58. Ramsey, *Ethics at the Edges of Life,* p. 145. Ramsey cites from Dyck's article that is cited in note 16.

59. *Ibid.*

60. On this see St. Thomas Aquinas, *Summa Theologiae,* 1-2, 94, 2. See Grisez, "The First Principle of Practical Reason; A Commentary on *Summa Theologiae,* 1-2, Q. 94, A. 2," *Natural Law Forum* 10 (1965) 168-201.

61. This is confirmed by the work of such developmental psychologists as Lawrence Kohlberg. On this see my "Natural Law, Conscience, and Developmental Psychology," *Communio* 2 (1975) 3-33. See also, on this matter, Piet Schoonenberg, *Man and Sin* (Notre Dame, Ind.: University of Notre Dame Press, 1965). Schoonenberg stresses that there is something positive in every sin.

62. Grisez argues that there are eight and only eight basic human goods. I do not believe that this is necessarily the case. The point is that *life* is one of the goods.

63. On real goods as a basis for human rights see Grisez and Boyle, *op. cit.,* chapter 1; see Jacques Maritain, *Man and the State* (Chicago: University of Chicago Press, 1965).

64. This is the point of St. Thomas in *Summa Theologiae,* 1-2, 94, 2.

65. On this see Ramsey's *War and Christian Conscience* (Durham, N.C.: Duke University Press, 1960).

66. It is rooted in *Summa Theologiae,* 2-2, 64, 7. On this principle see my article, "Double Effect, Principle of," in *Encyclopedia of Bioethics,* edited by Warren T. Reich (New York: Macmillan-Free Press, 1978).

67. For a good development of this see Grisez and Boyle, *op. cit.,* pp. 381-441.

68. This is the assertion made by Fletcher, among others. See "Ethics and Euthanasia," *loc. cit.,* 673. See also his *Morals and Medicine,* p. 211-212.

69. On this distinction see Dyck, *art. cit.;* Ramsey, "On (Only) Caring for the Dying," in his *Patient as Person.*

70. On this see my *Human Existence, Medicine, and Ethics,* pp. 146-147, with the literature cited there.

71. On Ramsey's proposals for using "medically indicated" and "medically nonindicated" see his *Ethics at the Edges of Life,* 153-159, 163-169 and passim.

72. For this criterion see Grisez and Boyle, *op. cit.,* pp. 414-417.

73. Elisabeth Kübler-Ross, *On Death and Dying* (New York: Macmillan, 1970), pp. 112-137, 157-180.

74. The ethic of Dr. Saunders and her associates is beautifully presented by R. Lamerton in *The Care of the Dying* (London: Priory Press, 1973).

75. *Gaudium et Spes,* n. 27.

76. In saying this I do not mean to imply that only explicit theists hold to this ethics. Many so-called nonbelievers might do so; but nonetheless there is implicit in this ethics a faith in God. On this see the first chapter of my *Becoming Human: An Invitation to Christian Ethics* (Dayton: Pflaum, 1974).

CATHOLIC PERSPECTIVES

The
Right
to
Die

PART TWO

by
Richard Westley

I

A Personal Preamble

THOUGH it is true that there are those who participate in the "right to die" dialogue with the same contentious spirit and rhetorical over-kill that marked the abortion controversy of the past decade, one senses in the current literature a real desire for dialogue, an honest search for consensus and a shared horror of the potential for tragedy which permeates "right to die" issues. But if the "right to die" discussion is carried on with respect and civility among academics, I have learned from recent experience that it is risky at best to even mention it to grass-roots Catholics. They are convinced either that the matter is definitively closed and beyond discussion, or that to publicly discuss it at this time in our history is unconscionable in the light of the current breakdown of morals.

While engaged in my most recent studies of the "right to die" question, I adopted the practice of attempting to discuss the matter with individual Catholics or with small private groups, trying, however informally, to get in touch with the *consensus fidelium.* Over a six month period I must have talked to over a hundred non-academic Catholics whose lives I take to be truly Christian. We talked about the propriety of ever taking direct action against innocent human life. Not once did a single one of them think that it was permissible even under the most compelling circumstances I could present. I am sorry to have to report that I have found absolutely no support among grass-roots Catholics for the position I will try to present in what follows. More than that, a close personal friend whose faith and goodness I know to be genuine urged me not to write on the subject, since he felt it would prove to be detrimental both to the Catholic community and to me personally. To make matters worse, others close to me concurred with that assessment.

From the start, I had known that it would be an awesome task to take on the entire Christian tradition of the West, but was prepared to attempt it in the interest of furthering the dialogue. Paradoxically, I found that I could not go against the members of the contemporary faith community with equal equanimity. There was some sort of lesson to be learned from the fact that I was less reluctant to stand opposed to the Fathers of the Church, St. Augustine, St. Cyprian, St. Ambrose, St. Irenaeus, St. Athanasius, St. Anselm, St. Thomas Aquinas, the Catholic theologians of the ages, the Code of Canon Law, and the Roman Pontiffs, than to stand opposed to the men and women with whom I share the Catholic faith in the Chicago Church of the fourth quarter of the 20th century. It became clear to me that learning that lesson would have to become an integral part of my project.

I had foreseen that by opposing the almost unanimous tradition of the Church regarding the absolute status of innocent human life I would be subject to the criticism that I was simply being anti-authority. I had long since made peace with myself over that issue primarily for two reasons. First, I do not reject that tradition but accept it as generally binding on all Catholics, in fact on all of humankind; still, I wanted to suggest that in practice it may be necessary "in faith" to act otherwise. And second, with the exception of the papal and concilar decrees and the Code of Canon Law, that Catholic tradition is contained in the writings, indeed the "academic" writings, of the great Christians of our past and as such is presented to the public forum for discussion and dialogue by believers. As an academic myself, I feel not only free but obliged to engage that tradition in creative dialogue from the perspective of contemporary faith.

What I had *not* foreseen and was totally unprepared for was the unanimous negative reaction from those fellow believers who knew me to be a person of faith and who even after hearing my case not only rejected it, but counselled me to be silent. By proceeding with the project, I was running the risk of appearing willful in callously ignoring the wise counsel of a prudent friend, that by so acting I would be doing real harm to the faith community. Suddenly, I was faced with the reality that I was not merely an academic but also a believer who was about to embark on something that was perceived by his fellows as harmful. Added to their sorrow and disappointment was the realization that my respect for and commitment to the *consensus fidelium* was bound to look inauthentic if I departed from it simply because it did not on this point agree with my own position. Coming to terms with all of that has proved to be personally much more difficult than coming to terms either with the tradition or with the "right to die" issues. My struggle with those difficulties came more and more to occupy my deliberations and has greatly shaped my account, taking it along unexpected paths. I had originally intended it to be a modest academic contribution to some aspect of the current "right to die" controversy, but found myself unable—no, unwilling—to settle for that. I had wisely or unwisely challenged my faith community on the "right to die" issue and they had in turn challenged me. If I was not going to heed their counsel to silence, then at least my account would be written with them, their concerns, and our shared faith very much in mind.

It may be too much to hope that what I have written will be seen by them as good, but because I have written it in faith and in fear and trembling, I will gladly settle for a final evaluation that it ultimately did not harm. In any case, that is for others to decide. As for myself, I did what I felt called to do, and am at peace.

II

Coming to Think the Unthinkable

YOU don't start out to stand over against your faith community; in fact, everything in you tends the other way. Even when a voice from deep within says that there is something not quite right, you look for any reason to remain faithful. For awhile you are successful in repressing it all and just don't think about it, but something eventually happens which makes it clear that you are going to have to face up to the inevitable. At that point you grieve a lot in silence. You grieve over your lost innocence. You grieve in anticipation of the alienation from life-giving roots and from the contemporary faith community which lies ahead. And you grieve over the precarious fallibility of the human mind, knowing that if and when you do speak out you can only do so in fear and trembling, never in certainty. At first you try to keep the burdensome secret to yourself, but eventually what lies hidden in the heart must be shouted from the housetops (Luke 12:2-3).

Identifying The Unthinkable

As a young college kid majoring in philosophy I had learned that there are really only three basic positions regarding the prolongation and/or termination of innocent human life. In the present context I will label them the *fundamentalist, liberal* and *radical* views, views which continue to set the perimeters within which the current "right to die" controversy is being argued out.

The FUNDAMENTALIST VIEW is unambiguous, straight-forward and admits of no exceptions. Human life is everywhere and under every imaginable circumstance an absolute good which as a gift from God is inviolably sacred. Everything possible must be done to prolong that life, regardless of its degree of vitality, since God alone has dominion over life and death. Our obligation is to sustain human life, without the slightest reservation, to the very end. Many mistakenly take this to be the "Catholic" position.

The official position of the Catholic Church is more appropriately designated as the LIBERAL VIEW, according to which human life is good but not absolutely so. Thus, though one is under no obligation to prolong it in any and every circumstance, because innocent human life is inviolably sacred one is never permitted to take direct action against it. What makes this view more "liberal" than the preceding one is the morally significant distinction between killing someone and allowing her to die. In the light of that distinction we are allowed both to suspend hopeless treatments and to refuse to undertake extraordinary ones, i.e., treatments which cannot be obtained or used without excessive expense, pain or other inconvenience. Liberals and the official Church hold that once the situation becomes hopeless, extraordinary means simply prolong the dying process and we are under no obligation at all to do that. But however much they may disagree on that point, the fundamentalists and the liberals remain in total agreement that under no circumstances may direct action be taken against innocent human life.

According to the RADICAL VIEW, it is generally true that it is immoral to take direct action against human life, but it is not absolutely true. There are situations and circumstances which invite and even compel us to act directly to terminate human life. The classic such case, then as now, is the situation in which a person in fact: a) is presently incurable; b) is beyond the aid of any cure or restoration which may reasonably be expected to become available within her life expectancy; c) is suffering intolerable and unmitigable pain; and d) is of a fixed and rational desire to die or has previously certified a wish to die in the event that the first three conditions should ever come to pass. It is precisely at that point that the "right to die," "death by choice" and "decision to die" advocates espouse taking direct action against human life. One reason the radical view is suddenly being urged so forcefully in our day is that the techniques of modern medicine have not only worked marvels for many, but they have also greatly increased the number of people who, unfortunately, find themselves in the classic situation described above.

I am sure that most of us, in former days, found that position a bit far-fetched. It was inconceivable to us that anyone serious about walking with the Lord would even be tempted to cross over the chasm separating believers from the advocates of euthanasia, much less actually make the move. Of course we had no way of knowing then that some thirty years later not only would many Catholics be making the move, but that some of us would be among their number. I know I didn't. How did I come to this? Why is it that, in mid-life after years of striving to be faithful, I have come to think the unthinkable thought? Have I after all, unwittingly, lost both my faith and my reason? Perhaps. But I must honestly say that I don't feel as if that is an accurate description of what has happened to me. Quite the contrary. It is only because of my conviction that at this stage of my life I am not only stronger in faith but also clearer about the role of reason in this matter that I found it possible to supervene the counsel to silence from friends and faith community. I cannot believe that there are not others who are struggling as I have, questioning their own faith and rationality over this question. My hope is that by sharing some of the key elements in my own personal struggle with the problem they may take heart from the knowledge that they are not alone.

Beginning To Question The Tradition

I remember, as a young boy in Milwaukee, seeing a sign in a German shoe repair shop which proclaimed: "Ve get so soon alt, and so late schmart." For some people even that is too optimistic a view: they live a very long time but *never* wise up. Experience may be the best teacher, but in order to be experience's pupil one has to be open to its lessons. That was especially difficult for the Catholics of my generation who felt little need for experience about such things as birth control, divorce and remarriage, abortion and mercy killing. Those matters, and many others, had been definitively settled by the tradition, supposedly on the basis of past experiences and revelations. When present experience contradicted what we had been taught we felt obliged to ignore our experience. But allowing our theology to shape our experience rather than seeing our experience as revelatory and allowing it to shape our theology was a major blunder.

Some Catholics, who at an earlier stage of their lives could not abide the thought of the direct termination of innocent human life, come to accept it as a possibility only after an experience with a terminally ill member of their own family. Even if they remain convinced that they themselves could never do such a thing, they are sympathetic and understanding of the consciences of those who could and can and do. Authentic human experiences have a way of transforming what we believe. As modern medical technology affords more and more Catholics first-hand experience of what terminal illness really entails, it will become increasingly difficult to keep them convinced that the radical view is really an immoral stance toward human life.

The Abraham Story

But direct personal experience with terminal illness is not the only way of coming to think the unthinkable. I suppose that as an academic it is fitting that for me the process should have begun in my head, and that as a Christian it began as I was thinking about Abraham, our father in faith. Not only was Abraham willing to kill his only son Isaac, but it is part of the tradition that it is precisely because of that fact that he is our father in faith. At the beginning of the fifth century, St. Augustine wrote with complete aplomb:

> However, there are some exceptions made by the divine authority to its own law, that men may not be put to

death. These exceptions are of two kinds, being justified either by a general law, or by a special commission granted for a time to some individual. And in this latter case, he to whom authority is delegated, and who is but the sword in the hand of him who uses it, is not himself responsible for the death he deals. . . . Abraham was thus not merely deemed guiltless . . . but even applauded for his piety.[1]

Traditionally then, there are two accepted exceptions to the prohibition against taking human life: cases of defense against unjust aggressors and the execution of criminals; and killing in obedience to a direct command from God, who alone has dominion over life and death. Eight hundred years after Augustine, Thomas Aquinas was teaching the same thing;[2] and five hundred years after Aquinas, Soren Kierkegaard, while writing a brilliant account of the existential anxiety which such a command from God must have caused Abraham, dubs him a "knight of faith" and criticizes his contemporaries for thinking their way around him.[3]

This time when studying the Abraham story, I remember thinking to myself: If God appeared to me and asked me to kill one of my kids, I'd tell him to bug off! "If you want to get someone to kill my son, you'd better get yourself another boy, I won't do it. After all I'm the lad's *father.* Besides, if you're so insensitive as to make that sort of demand of me, then I know you're a fraud, you're *not* the Lord!" If, as I to this day remain convinced, that is what Abraham should have said, if, indeed, that is what any person of authentic faith would say, why, as our father in faith, didn't Abraham say it? (In due time I came to understand why, but that gets us ahead of ourselves in the account of my journey.)

As now seems clear to me, it was this little episode which started me down the road toward the radical view. Granted that nothing in that thought process touched directly on the "right to die," it nonetheless made me suspicious of the traditional account of how God relates to humankind.

Life As Gift

One robin does not a Spring make—so one thought-episode does not a whole tradition undo. Traditional perspectives may perhaps be overturned suddenly by a profound enough experience, but when one is being led intellectually to question that tradition it is less accurate to speak of its being overturned than to speak of its being slowly and quietly eroded. The next tradition-eroding intellectual episode occurred when I was writing a book on the "right to life,"[4] and preparing a class in pastoral theology entitled *Celebrate the Gift*. This time it was Thomas Aquinas who sparked the reflection. In listing his reasons for thinking suicide was forbidden, he wrote:

> To kill oneself is never allowed because life is a gift to man from God who alone has the authority to kill and to give life. Hence whoever takes his own life sins against God in the same way that he who kills another's slave sins against the slave's master, and as he sins who takes on himself for judgment a matter not entrusted to him.[5]

Once again I was in the presence of a text which I had accepted without question for years, but this time the phrase "life is a gift to man from God" seemed strangely troublesome. Either life is given us by God as a gift, in which case it is ours and ours unconditionally,

or we are given life the way the servants in Luke 19:
11-27 were given money, which means life is never
truly ours but merely temporarily entrusted to us. Now
it is difficult to see how the tradition can have it both
ways. Either we hold our lives as stewards, and then it is
strange to call it gift, or life is truly a gift, in which case
the notion of stewardship seems grossly misapplied.

I frankly admit that it seems better to me to hold on
to the notion of life as a "gift" or "grace" from God
rather than to extend the notion of "stewardship" to the
very life of the self. But that forces one to raise the difficult question: If life is a gift from God, why is a person
not at liberty to dispose of that gift as *she* chooses?
Aquinas seemed ready with an answer, for in that same
text he remarked:

> That a person has dominion over himself is because he
> is endowed with free choice. Thanks to that free choice
> a man is at liberty to dispose of himself with respect to
> those things in this life which are subject to his freedom.
> But the passage from this life to a happier one is not one
> of those things, for one's passage from this life is subject
> to the will and power of God.[6]

Obviously, Aquinas thinks that human freedom extends
"to the things of life" but not to life itself. But this attempt to limit human freedom comes a little too late
in his argument. If one holds that life is a gift, already
implicit in that notion of "gift" is that that with which
I am gifted is precisely by that fact made subject to my
freedom. By calling life a "gift from God," Aquinas was
precluding the possibility of his effectively using the
argument about the limitation of human freedom to
show why a man or woman may never take their own

lives. I could not help but wonder at that point: If that is so clear to me, why was it not clear to Aquinas?

I was now, more than ever, convinced that there was something terribly wrong-headed about the tradition, and I was beginning to feel sorry for God. He was taking a bum rap because of the way we Christians talked about him. Not only did we depict him as capable of asking a father to kill his own son just to test the father's obedience but we also insisted on portraying his gifts as conditional, thus making them appear more like bribes than the pure gratuities of love they are. And so it was that, almost without realizing it, I had come to find myself squared off against the whole Christian tradition and on the verge of thinking what, in my younger days, I would have told anyone was unthinkable.

III

To Kill or Not To Kill?

IF thought-episodes such as those mentioned in the preceding section tend to erode one's confidence in the tradition and in the liberal view, concrete cases can often present a much more direct challenge. In my private little canvass of the Catholic community, along with my intellectual suspicions, I presented three concrete cases, two of which I took to be "knock-down" cases sure to elicit a "permission to kill." The third case was less clear but was used by me to insure further dialogue on the problem. As I have already indicated, there was dialogue aplenty, but no one I spoke to thought it permissible to kill, not even in my "knock-down" cases. Those cases, and the responses to them by grass-roots Catholics, reveal key elements of their theological perspective as well as the genuine fears and anxieties they feel over the "right to die" issue.

Three Concrete Cases

The first case is hypothetical but by no means unrealistic, and I take it to be the clearest sort of case of permissible direct or voluntary euthanasia.

Case #1: *The Trapped Truck Driver*

A truck driver hauling dangerous flammables is forced to swerve sharply to avoid an accident. In the process his truck overturns and bursts into flames. He is trapped in the cab of his truck as the flames get closer. It is clear that the fire engines will be several more minutes in coming and by then the driver will be consumed by the flames. The police arrive but because the heat and flames are so intense they can do little more than hold back the crowd. From inside the cab the trapped driver yells out to a policeman: "For Christ's sake, don't let me roast to death. Shoot me!"

Whatever the legal consequences of an officer's shooting the driver in those circumstances, it seems clear to me that he would not be acting immorally were he to grant the driver's last request. More than that, I think a good case could be made "in faith" that what Christian charity might require in that situation is precisely what the Christian tradition deems to be unthinkable.

The second case is an actual case which received national notoriety in 1971[7] and which was ultimately settled along liberal lines. It became notorious and controversial because it seemed clear to some that it might better have been settled along radical lines[8] and to others that it was a gross misunderstanding and misapplication of liberal principles.[9] It is both more ambiguous and less acceptable than the truck driver case because it is an instance of involuntary euthanasia of a defective infant.

Case #2: *The Johns Hopkins Baby Case*

At the Johns Hopkins University Hospital, a mongoloid (Down's syndrome) baby was born with no connection between his stomach and his small intestine. Surgery was required if the child was to survive. The parents, proceeding on the principle that they were not obliged to take extraordinary means to save the life of an already defec-

71

tive child, refused to give their permission. When it was determined through legal counsel that the courts would probably not order the operation against the parents' wishes in light of the child's mental defect, the doctors reluctantly invoked the same no extraordinary means principle. They ordered that no intravenous feedings be given and because the child could not take food orally it was simply allowed to starve to death in the hospital—an agonizing spectacle for the staff which took some 15 days.

That was how that tragic scenario ended, but it does not take any imagination at all to see that another time the case might very easily end this way:

The nursery staff was greatly agitated and distraught over having to stand by and watch the baby starve to death. Finally, on the sixth day, one of the nurses could stand it no longer. She gave the infant a fatal dose of morphine on the principle that killing the child was more merciful and humane than allowing it to die that way.

Now while it might be possible in this case to fault the parents and the doctors, I myself would judge the hypothetical nurse in this case to have done a good and godly act under the circumstances.

The third case proved to be the most troublesome of the three for my Catholic friends. I think that this is because it most directly challenges Christian values. At least that is why I am more troubled by it than either of the other two. (Or is it perhaps because the people involved in this actual case are personally known to me?)

Case #3: *A Long-Term Quadraplegic*

A young man of twenty injured his neck in an accident so severely that he was totally paralyzed from the neck down. His family rallied around him in his hour of tragic need, and his brother strove to re-enkindle hope in his stricken younger brother. As the months and years went by, he tried to get his brother to see that he could still have meaningful relationships, that he could still be a sign of the Kingdom, and that he could touch and gift others with his spirit. Finally, the younger lad had had enough. He said to his brother: "I wish I could be the person of faith you want me to be. But I am no hero. I simply do not want to live this way, and I would kill myself if only I could, but I can't." It is almost six years since the accident, and the young man remains of that mind. Will a time ever come when it would be proper for the Christian community to answer his request?

This case is beyond the ken of most of us because it represents despairing of human life in the face of adversity, the so-called unforgiveable sin. It goes against that which is quintessentially Christian: hope and trust in God. We are ill prepared to face up to the implications of this case because, as Catholics, we have been over-fed a theology of sin and are totally lacking what is so desperately needed in this cruel and imperfect world, a theology of failure.[10] Because we are so accustomed to identifying failure with sin, we don't know where to begin to give people permission to fail. So we find ourselves preferring that the young man in the third case live out his life for forty or fifty years as a quadraplegic, even if he does so grudgingly and in absolute bitterness. We shall work and hope and pray for his own conversion to hope, we shall talk piously of the "will of God," but we cannot abide his despair or surrender to despair ourselves by giving up our hope in him. No one for a moment denies the nobility of such an approach. That is not what is being questioned. The question is: Is forcing an unwanted heroism on the helpless really the only option open to Christians?

The Community Responds

By taking this matter and these cases to believing Catholics and by insisting that they dialogue with me over the "right to die" issue, I have undoubtedly caused them pain. They were, nonetheless, never anything but gracious and patient with my attempt to get them to see the inevitability of the radical view. I am most grateful for their forbearance and want publicly to thank each and every one of them. (They will know who they are.) But most of all, I want to thank them for their sensitivity and wisdom in commenting on our three cases. I always came away from such dialogues enriched, and more keenly aware than ever that there are at least two sides to every story and that this fact puts a tremendous responsibility on anyone who dares to discuss such delicate matters in print.

The Catholics with whom I spoke were by and large unimpressed by the truck driver case, which is to say it didn't elicit from them the slightest sense of urgency. God alone has dominion over life and death, and that settled the matter for them. But leaving the divine dominion point aside, it seemed as clear to them that there was really no need to shoot the driver as it was clear to me that it was morally permissible to do so. Beyond that, they reminded me that it might even be harmful to shoot him, depending on the state of his soul.

As to why they felt there was no need to shoot, two reasons were most often given. First, no one has a right to ask such a thing of another human being, therefore one is under no obligation whatsoever to comply with such requests. And second, even though his suffering would be intense, mercifully it would be short-lived and his death would be very quick. In that context, one woman sadly remarked: "He should thank God he died that way. He got just enough time to make peace with God and then died quickly. My husband prayed for such a death. Instead, he lingered for years with painful cancer, and was something less than human when he finally succumbed." With great wisdom the community was reminding me that in such matters as these the time/duration factor is extremely important. Their conclusion was that, while tragic, the entire truck driver incident was so sudden and of so short duration that it scarcely warrants being raised to the level of moral dilemma.

As befits a people called to be in and of the world but not to place their ultimate hope in the worldly, the Catholics I spoke to invariably expressed genuine concern for the state of the driver's soul. If it was unthinkable to shoot him, the thought of killing him in the state of deadly sin and thus of depriving him of the chance at repentance his suffering would offer was a possibility too frightening to contemplate. Since there was no way to realistically determine whether the man was in mortal sin or not, it was out of the question that he be dispatched by a bullet. A few people felt additional reluctance to interfere because they did not know the kind of life the driver led prior to the accident. There was always the possibility that the fiery crash was a punishment from God for past offenses and so to interfere would be to short-circuit divine justice.

Finally, as also befits a people called to live by hope

75

and trust in God, there is always the ever present possibility of a miracle, be it a sudden cloud-burst or a divine intervention of even more spectacular dimensions. To take the matter into one's own hands seems contrary to the Christian vocation to put such things in the hands of God.

The second case, of the mongoloid baby left to starve to death in the hospital nursery, generated an entirely different set of responses from this same group of Catholics. I was struck by the fact that the parents and the culture came to be the centers of attention; my hypothetical nurse was simply ignored. They took this case as an opportunity to give voice to their concerns about the current attitude toward family and human life in our culture.

The case as presented does not give any information about the degree of retardation which was diagnosed as likely for the child. As it so happens, the Johns Hopkins child would have been appreciably retarded but would have been able to relate to his environment and enter into simple relationships with those about him. He would have been neither vegetable nor monstrosity, but rather a severely retarded human being. Once supplied with that knowledge, the verdict was unanimous. The parents had invoked the "no extraordinary means" principle to relieve themselves of a burden, not to relieve the child. If they had had real concern for the child they would not have condemned him to so tortured a death. They were primarily concerned with themselves.

More often than not, equally harsh judgments were made about the current trend to think of children as a burden much better avoided. If that's the prevailing attitude toward healthy children, it is small wonder that defective ones are dispatched without further ado. Given the way we already treat the elderly, the sick and the poor; given the fact that the energy crisis, inflation and rising medical costs all threaten the American standard of living; and given the fact that the number of poor and elderly are likely to double in the next twenty years, how can we be sure that the sudden concern with euthanasia is not due to expediency and self-interest? Is it safe or prudent to even discuss the direct taking of innocent human life in a culture like ours where we've turned the care of the elderly into a business and the delivery of health services into an industry in each of which profit is the paramount value?[11] I was fraternally warned against writing in favor of euthanasia because by doing so I would be contributing to the cultural malaise of egoism and self indulgence. As a Christian how could I ever contemplate doing such a thing?

The response I got to the third case, the long term quadraplegic, was equally impassioned and equally wise. As in the first case, time seemed to loom important in the discussion. Despair is more often than not only a temporary state of mind. Like anger, it cannot be sustained indefinitely. It will eventually yield to the loving care and concern of the community. The obligation of the Christian in this case is to be patient and to not act precipitously. Perhaps others can help the lad come to renewed hope where his own brother failed. Besides, there is clinical evidence that in cases of quadraplegia a period of dark despair lasting for as long as five or six years is entirely normal. If that knowledge sustains therapists in their efforts, how much more ought we Christians to persevere hopefully in our own efforts?

To accede to the request of the quadraplegic is so much a counter sign to what Christianity is all about, that it is out of the question to even consider it. Once trust in God and in one another no longer enlivens human relationships, human life is so degraded that it can no longer be a sign of the Kingdom, nor witness to the creative possibilities of life which the Lord incarnated and came to secure for all. In the tragic circumstances presented in the third case, the only viable option for the Christian community is to be faithful to its vocation to be a sign of hope.

Finally, leaving all these considerations aside, even if one could justify our acting directly against human life, who would do it? Who could be trusted to do it? No one could attempt such an action with relish. So in this culture we'd probably end up paying someone to do it and before you knew it we'd have professional terminators. And before long there would be a business set up with ads in the Yellow Pages, just as we have for abortions, and profit and self interest would once again come to govern the enterprise. While others may wish to go that route, and while it is very likely that our country will eventually go that route and legalize euthanasia, the Christian community must stand opposed to such foolishness or cease to be. That is, it will be neither community, nor Christian.

Summing Up

The high quality of the community's response can scarcely be denied. No wonder I have had both my faith and my reason impugned because I want to question the foundations of the liberal position. And that, in the end, is all that I mean to do. I agree with most of what my community has said, and want to bring into question not the whole of our shared values, but only the two pillars on which the liberal position rests, namely that

God alone has dominion over life and death; and that it is never justified to take direct action against innocent human life. In fact, I am surprised that this has proven so controversial, since I feel that any Christian who really takes heed of herself and lives long enough, inevitably comes to know not only that the unthinkable is thinkable, but that it is also true. In the end, however, no matter how we come at the problem, be it from faith or from reason, it is important for us to recall the fallibility of the human condition and the seriousness of the issue.

> Taking the life of another human being regardless of the circumstances, is a grave and dangerous act. It is the counsel of wisdom that we shall never have reflected on such an act sufficiently to enter into it with perfect certainty that it should be committed. Similarly, we can never decide wih perfect certainty that there is no circumstance in which euthanasia is not acceptable.[12]

Whatever our position, we can but adopt it in fear and trembling.

IV

Justifying the Unthinkable

SOME things are literally "unthinkable" because they are self-contradictory, which is why the human mind is unable to deliver them to consciousness. We may be able to label such things with words, but then the words are merely tokens and not names, because the self-contradictory not only does not and cannot exist in reality, it cannot even be made to exist in thought. To say "square-circle" is, therefore, really neither to speak, to name, nor to think.

Other things are only metaphorically "unthinkable" in the sense that though they are not self-contradictory, they do contradict other propositions which a person holds to be true in her worldview, her value system, or her moral perspective. It is in this second sense that euthanasia is unthinkable to most Catholics.

More specifically, to say that in some cases it is morally permissible for a creature to take direct action against innocent human life contradicts the two unassailable propositions which form, for Catholics, the very foundation of the liberal view. They are: (1) That God alone has absolute dominion over life and death; and (2) That all direct killing of the innocent is morally wrong. In the present context, to justify the unthinkable means to attempt to justify the opposing propositions that: (A) According to Christian faith dominion over life and death is *not* the sole prerogative of God; and that (B) Direct killing of the innocent is in some instances not only morally permissible but even morally commendable. The prospects for success in such an endeavor are understandably slim. Since propositions (A) and (B) contradict other things dear to Catholics, accepting them as "justified" will require a Catholic to not only give up propositions (1) and (2) which form the foundation of the liberal view, but also to give up those other things in her religious overview which propositions (A) and (B) contradict. (Obviously, as I now see after my experience with my community, the likelihood of that happening in the near future is very small. Still, one must make a beginning.[13])

Having identified the unthinkable, we may now ask what it would mean "to justify" it. According to the dictionary, the first meaning of "to justify" is "to show something to be just, to be right, and in accord with reason." As a philosophy teacher, I have pondered long and hard on that simple definition and have been unable to completely satisfy myself about it. My problem is this. It makes perfectly good sense to say that whatever is just is right, and whatever is right is just. It even makes sense to say that whatever is right and just is in accord with reason. What makes no sense is saying, as many seem to, that whatever is in accord with reason is right and just. If, as I think, that is not true, then the possibility is left open that one might well show that something is in accord with reason and still not really "justify" it in the sense of showing it to be right or just. Consequently, in the current "right to die" discussions, those who attempt to show that euthanasia is in accord with reason are met with the response from some Catholics that even so—it just is not right.[14]

The truth is that no matter how much we Christians

might wish it were otherwise, "reason" alone does not, and indeed cannot, give Christian morality anything like total support or invulnerable protection. This is especially true in the "right to life" and "right to die" issues. Joseph Sullivan, a moral theologian holding strictly to the traditional Catholic view, was obliged to write in 1950:

> It must be admitted candidly that without the support of the teaching Church, Revelation and the general heritage of the West, it is difficult to establish from reason alone that mercy killing, especially voluntary mercy killing, is always under every condition illicit. Though the argument from reason is objectively good, it requires more than reason to present a proof that will carry conviction to all.[15]

All of which conjures up the picture of the participants in the "right to die" discussions eventually coming to a rational stalemate, at which time the believer takes out her trump cards—Revelation, the teaching Church, and the Christian heritage of the West—to win the day. Of course, in reality it turns out quite differently. Since the discussions take place in the public forum, they are conducted on the basis of the rules which govern such discussions in a pluralistic society,[16] consequently the believer's trump cards never get admitted to the game. That means that in a pluralistic society the "right to die" discussions must inevitably end in a stalemate or standoff. The parties simply agree to disagree, but they don't stop talking because each side is anxious to convert the younger members of the society to its banner.

The stalemate or standoff is a real disappointment to Catholics in whose tradition "reason" plays so important a role. Surely Aquinas spoke for the whole Catholic tradition when he wrote: "Human morality is spoken of as being ordained to reason which is the proper principal of human acts. Those acts are called morally good when they conform to reason, and morally evil when they depart from it."[17] But if, as we have seen, the arguments over mercy killing cannot be settled definitively from reason alone, and if there are reasonable persons on both sides of that issue, what are we to do?

First, we would do well to recall that in the Catholic tradition conformity to reason alone is *not* the norm of morality. For Aquinas also said: ". . . human acts are considered good or evil depending on whether they conform to a reason informed by divine law either naturally, by instruction or by infusion."[18] Robert Johann put that thought in contemporary language when he wrote: "The morally right is not what conforms to determinate nature but what conforms to the dictates of a reason enlisted in love's service."[19] In all disputes over Christian morality it is reason informed by virtue and love which is the adequate norm. That is why I have consistently held that it would be better for us Christians to say virtue is the norm of morality.[20] That might well disqualify us from participation in the public forum in this culture, but it would have the advantage of being closer to the truth.

Secondly, we should get clear on just what it is that reason can deliver. We Catholics have, by and large, failed to distinguish those things which are *required by reason* from those which are merely *allowed by reason.*[21] Because of that failure many think that what is in accord with reason is always morally right. The truth of the matter is that many things which reason allows are contradictory to the Christian ethos. It is never irrational for a person to act in her own self interest. When I am caught stealing a TV set, no one says that I acted in an irrational way, only that what I did rationally was immoral. On the other hand, reason cannot require me to always act solely out of self interest. It is perfectly rational to act against self-interest for a good enough reason. Never is it irrational for a person to lay down her life for her friend, but neither is it irrational to let the friend die in order to save one's own life. Reason cannot insist that one *must* lay down her life for her friend because to act in one's own interest is always rational. The most reason can deliver in this matter is the judgment that should one choose to lay down her life for her friend, such an action is neither irrational nor unreasonable. Reason then is constitutionally unable either to impose the high ideals of Christianity as norms of conduct, or to forbid acting in accord with such ideals because they go against self-interest.

Our Christian ideals are said to be in accord with reason, then, only in the limited sense that they are allowed and *not* required by reason. So, though reason allows one to accept the excruciating sufferings of a terminal illness in the name of the Lord, i.e., it is not unreasonable to do so, reason also allows one who is terminally ill to kill herself or ask to be killed since it is never irrational to act out of self interest. In the absence of a requirement from reason, we are at liberty to choose any one of the many alternatives which reason allows and still be judged reasonable and rational in our action. Clearly, under such circumstances no amount of rational argumentation is going to be able

to settle the "right to life" or the "right to die" issues.
Those debates, I fear, are destined to go on forever.

That does not mean that we should give up all attempts at rational justification of our positions, but it
does mean that we shall have to settle for arguments
which can only show that our personal positions are
allowed by reason, knowing full well that the positions
of our opponents are too. And since reason abides on
both sides of the argument, reason does not allow us to
argue that those who do not agree with us are, for that
reason alone, being either stupid or irrational.

"To justify" something means showing that it is "in
accord with reason" either because reason requires it,
or because reason allows it. Justification, then, can have
either a strong or a weak sense. In this section, my
attempt at justifying the unthinkable should be interpreted as an attempt at justification in its weaker sense.
Does reason allow a *Christian* to hold that dominion
over life and death is not the sole prerogative of God?
Does reason allow a *Christian* to hold that direct killing
of the innocent is in some instances morally permissible? Is it irrational for *Christians* to hold such things?
And even if reason allows us to hold such things, does
our "faith" allow it? From the start it has been clear
that I think the answer to all those questions is affirma-
tive. The time has come for me to give my reasons.

Proposition (1): The Divine Dominion Principle

In the "right to die" literature, discussions eventually
come to a point at which the author says: "Religious
considerations aside . . ."; or "Passing over the theological suppositions. . . ." Because the debate is carried
on solely from the perspective of reason, faith and

religion are usually left out of consideration. That strategy is not open to us if we are to call the foundations of the liberal view into question. The main pillar on which that view rests is the *religious* conviction that God alone has dominion over life and death. Getting around that might not be as impossible as first appears, especially should it turn out that Christianity is not a religion.

Faith vs. Religion

It is widely assumed by Catholics that "religion" and "faith" are the same thing, but they are not. What makes them look alike is that each is a particular way for humankind to relate to the divine. Their difference stems from the fact that in "religion" and "faith" we relate to the divine in diametrically opposed ways. One reason we have found it so difficult to distinguish them is that they are never isolated or separate, but have, from the first moment faith came upon the scene, been joined or mixed together. And even today it is hard to tell them apart, and much of what looks like renewal is actually, on closer inspection, a resurgence of religiosity, not faith.

We get a good insight into the basic difference between faith and religion if we examine their maxims. The maxim of religion is: "Fear not, trust in God and he will see to it that none of the things you fear will happen to you." But the maxim of the person of faith is: "Fear not, the things you are afraid of are likely to happen to you, but they are really nothing to be afraid of and have very little significance compared to transforming the world into the Kingdom."

Religions are created by human beings for the same reason we fashion anything else, to meet a particular human need. Beset as we are with the uncertainties of life, the painful struggle to grow and mature as we fashion our lives into something truly meaningful, the inevitability of failure, suffering, aging and death, it is only natural for us to seek help in coping. One reason for the continuing popularity of religion among the world's peoples is that religion remains to this very day the most satisfactory way of coping with those problems, even in an unbelieving age like ours. Put simply, religion is natural to humankind and is a product of our fear and self-interest. Whenever we relate to God out of fear or self-interest, we can be sure that the relationship is a religious one. Left to ourselves we seem incapable of relating to God other than religiously.

But happily, we have not been left to ourselves. The call to Abraham, our father in faith, was the call to leave not only his homeland but also to give up religion by answering the call to faith. Ever since, and throughout the long history of the Judaeo-Christian tradition, the constant voice of Yaweh, the Faithful One, can be heard sounding in the lives and experiences of his people, inviting them to give up the demeaning, counterfeit benefits of "religion" and to freely embrace the much more demanding ideal of "incarnational faith." For so long as we relate to God as a way of coping with the vicissitudes of life, we have not yet arrived at the realm of faith.

Faith is not a man-made relationship to God out of human self-interest. It is rather the unbelievable relationship which the Lord God initiated with our race for a divine purpose. We got some indication of that purpose when Yaweh called Abraham to faith. "Look around you, Abraham, things are not as they should be. Everything is out of joint, it is *not* my dream, it does *not* speak my presence, leave it all and start anew. And if you do, I shall be your God and YOU SHALL BE MY PEOPLE."

Later, we got another clue to that purpose when Yaweh called Moses to go to Egypt to free the children of Israel. Moses asked, "How shall they know that it is you who sent me? What shall I say to them?" And God said, "Tell them that He who is with them, He who walks with them and is present in their midst as he promised their father, Abraham, it is *He* who sends you. For I am the-God-with-his-people, the God of Freedom, I am Yaweh, the Faithful One."

For centuries the descendants of Abraham and Moses were the laughing stock of the ancient world. Their neighbors always thought them rather strange and particularly irreligious because they carried around the Ark of the Covenant and thought that God actually dwelt with them. After centuries of such ridicule, their "faith" was at long last validated as the Word became flesh and dwelt among us. But the misunderstanding did not cease, not even among the disciples. After being with the Lord for years, Philip walked up to him one day and asked: "Lord when are you going to show us the Father?" And Jesus said, "Philip, you're looking at him, the Father and I are one." But in saying that, Jesus was revealing not only who he was, but also who we are. For Jesus was saying to Philip that God is not to be found outside of humankind, but within, in the intimacy and togetherness of man and God, promised and foretold in the Covenant, effected and realized in the Lord Jesus, and present in each one of us when we truly walk with him in faith.

So for the first time the secret of faith was fully revealed in and by the Lord. God is human not only in Christ Jesus, he is human in each one of us and was from the very beginning, only no one would believe him when he tried to reveal it. With the coming of Christ, we now know definitively where God is. He is not in religious images, laws or rituals; he is not in Jerusalem, Mecca or even Rome. He is not in some far off heaven. No, he is where he has always been, with, among and in his people, especially in our noblest parts where justice and charity dwell. Contrary to what "religious" Christians may say, *that* is the Good News of the Gospel, *that* is what communally funded human experience constantly reveals. One becomes a person of "faith" only by accepting and responding to *that* truth. The implementation of that truth is what Scripture calls the Reign of God, or the Coming of the Kingdom.

Faith, unlike religion, is not centered on our getting something from God. The call to faith is the call to give ourselves wholeheartedly to God's great dream for our world. That more than anything else is what distinguishes Christianity from religions. Religions ultimately despair of this world, all their hopes lie in another, higher, better world beyond this one, to which religious people will ultimately retire in peace and joy if they religiously perform the prescribed rites. It is or should be, quite otherwise with us Christians.

Our God not only became one of us, he lives in this

world, dwells in our noblest parts, and is at work transforming this world into the Kingdom. He has promised that one day *this* world, the world of war, injustice, racism, sexism, violence, drug abuse, pornography, suffering, death and self-seeking religion will *be* the Kingdom. People of faith believe that so strongly that they can't wait for it to happen, and so freely take on the Christian mission and ministry to live the Gospel values *now* as a sign of hope to others—others who will be convinced that the Kingdom the Lord promised really is coming and is no idle daydream because they will see it actually emerging in us. The Coming of that Kingdom, not the saving of our souls, is the major concern of "incarnational faith."

But being human, we have always found pure faith just a bit too much for us. Our fear of life, our terror of death, and our anxiety about the hereafter have always tempted us to mix ever larger doses of religion with our faith. Even the writers of the Old and New Testaments can't seem to keep religion out of their faith stories. Their accounts alternate between a God in whose presence we are but dust and to whom we owe religious obedience, and a God who becomes human and reveals himself as Father, declaring the adoption of our race to a divine status. The point, of course, is that Scripture may be read either way. And because it can, one cannot invoke those Scriptures to settle the dispute as to whether Christianity is more authentically interpreted as a religion or a faith. Believers must themselves choose whether to see the Scriptures as a call to religion or faith. And in doing so, they will inevitably have recourse to their own experiences. Is the God who is revealed there the God of religion or the God of faith? Put another way, in answering the call to keep faith with the Catholic tradition, we are going to have to decide whether that means keeping faith with the religious elements of that tradition or with its faith elements. It is impossible for us to do full justice to both.

What should be clear from all of this is that faith and religion are like the wheat and the weeds (Cf. Matt. 13:24-30), they co-exist not only in each of our individual lives, but throughout the whole of Scripture and Tradition as well. But if, like the sower of the seed, we are unable to separate them at this time, then, also like the sower, we had better be able to recognize which is which or we shall make some terrible blunders come harvest time.

Faith and Divine Dominion

What, you may ask, does all this have to do with divine dominion, much less with the "right to die"? We are constantly being told that the reason we do not have a "right to die" is because life and death are under the exclusive dominion of God. And so they are—*in the religious version of the story*. Though that story of divine dominion may be an essential ingredient in the religious account of Christianity, it is unnecessary and even foreign to incarnational faith. Incarnation means, among other things, that the divine and human are inextricably wedded to one another and that with respect to acting in the world it is bootless to talk of divine vs. human prerogatives. Through incarnation God has freely chosen to make his work our own, and it is in and through faith that we accept the challenge. If one still insists, in this context, of speaking of God's dominion over life and death, then thanks to incarnation that dominion is in some way also ours, since he lives in us.

The religious revival among fundamentalist Christians notwithstanding, few, if any, of us have ever experienced God as the Supreme Being who intervenes dramatically *in* our lives. We have no experience of the religious God of power and might who is our over-against, who resides in a world apart and who intermittently intervenes in our lives as he wills. And yet we are told to wait on such a God—refraining from any direct action against innocent human life. But to think that one must await his intervention is faithless because it is to suggest that he is somehow absent, or if present, inactive. The God of our experience is rather the quiet God of intimacy who *is* our very lives. We become aware of his presence when our minds are illumined, our hearts kindled, our lives strengthened, renewed and touched by the power of love. When that happens we find ourselves empowered to act, and if that is really what has happened, our act is unquestionably godly. But we can only claim that in fear and trembling awaiting confirmation from the faith-community.

Unfinished Business

The limitations of space have prevented my doing more than sketch with broad strokes the sorts of moves a believer might make against the divine dominion argument. Much more could, and should, be said. My only purpose has been to show that it is neither contradictory nor irrational for a Christian to reject the divine dominion argument. One can do it and remain a Christian, but not a "religious" one.

I think the reflection on faith and religion allows us to attempt answers to those questions asked earlier on. If Abraham was our father in "faith," why didn't he tell God to bug off when he asked for Isaac's life? That is, in a way, the wrong question. It is not a question of Abraham, but of why the Old Testament writers told his story the way they did. Their principal aim was to show that human sacrifice was not to occur in Israel. Everything else in their story was secondary to that. Then too, because the Old Testament writers were not always clear on the difference between faith and religion, they often identified the two. This they did in the Abraham story—thus making Abraham our father in faith for an act of religious obedience. That confusion has occasioned the spilling of much ink as thinkers throughout the ages have attempted to justify in Abraham what is truly unthinkable. This does not mean that Abraham is not our father in faith, but rather that he is not our father in faith for the reason given in the Old Testament. (I leave it to the reader to discern what really earned him that title.)

Aquinas was prevented from seeing the implications of calling life a "gift," namely, that it was ours to dispose of as we will, because he held the divine dominion principle. He did not think there was any way around it, and so was not open to seeing what was before his very eyes.

The same is true of the Christian tradition. It is adamant about no direct killing of innocent human life because it holds fast to the divine dominion principle. But it will not do to say that we cannot go against that principle because it is traditional with Christians. As has been shown, that principle is part of our "religious," not "faith," tradition. Failure to make that distinction was also what caused my community to question my faith. They would have been closer to the mark had they questioned my religion. For as must by now be abundantly clear, I gladly admit to the charge of being irreligious.

Proposition (2): The No Direct Killing Principle

As already noted, the liberal view rests on two foundational propositions. The second, the no direct killing of the innocent principle, is really a derivative from the first, the divine dominion principle. Deprived of the support of the religious divine dominion principle, the no direct killing principle is forced to stand or fall in the public forum by the support it can garner from reason. In such circumstances, its prospects have never been very bright. In 1516, no less eminent a Catholic than St. Thomas More portrayed the "right to die" as in accord with reason and love. In Book II of his classic account of a mythical and truly humanistic community, *Utopia,* he wrote:

> If a disease is not only incurable but also distressing and agonizing without any cessation, then the priests and the public officials exhort the man, since he is now unequal to all life's duties, a burden to himself, and a trouble to others, and is living beyond the time of his death, to make up his mind not to foster the pest and plague any longer nor to hesitate to die now that life is a torture to him but, relying on good hope, to free himself from this bitter life as from prison and the rack, or else voluntarily to permit others to free him. In this course he will act wisely, since by death he will put an end not to enjoyment but to torture. Because in doing so he will be obeying the counsels of the priests, who are God's interpreters, it will

be a pious and holy action. Those who have been per-
suaded by these arguments either starve themselves to
death or, being put to sleep, are set free without the sen-
sation of dying. *But they do not make away with anyone
against his will,* nor in such a case do they relax in the
least their attendance upon him. They believe that death
counseled by authority is honorific.[22]

Thomas More is indeed, as Robert Bolt suggests, a man
for all seasons. His statement of over 450 years ago still
captures the best of what so many call for today: Un-
relenting care and concern for the dying to the end;
respect for their personhood and freedom, the need for
counsel with the community in arriving at a decision,
respect for that decision once made, and a strong belief in the individual's "right to die."

And in our own day, the prospects for the no direct
killing principle are no brighter. Since ours is a pluralistic culture, the current debate on that issue is being
carried on without the support of any religious principles. Such principles have no place in a public forum
which is secular. Consequently, believers who choose
to participate in the current discussions are forced to
argue the case of the no direct killing principle on its
own merits. This accounts for a growing literature
which abounds with intellectual machinations by philosophers and theologians as they argue pro and con on
the issue of whether killing of the innocent is ever permissible; and whether in the light of the Johns Hopkins
case and others like it, the distinction between killing
and letting die continues to have moral significance.[23]
Though both sides are ably represented and their dialogue is serious, intelligent and interesting, I have a
feeling that the proponents of the principle are slowly

but irrevocably losing ground. That was inevitable once reason became the sole arbiter, for as we have already seen, theologians themselves admit that the arguments from reason against euthanasia are not adequate. There seems to be little doubt that eventually the position of Thomas More and his contemporary cohorts[24] will be judged the pre-eminently rational one and will carry the day among Catholic intellectuals. It is merely a matter of time.

But as I learned from recent experience, the Catholic community at large remains firm in its adherence to the liberal position. Yet even among ordinary Catholics two cases have had a tremendous impact and have begun to erode confidence in the no direct killing principle. In the abortion debate of the past decade, one question which exercised both sides was whether in the life against life situation, when killing either the fetus or the mother was the only way to save the other, it was permissible to take direct action against innocent life. The response from proponents of the no direct killing principle was that both mother and child must be allowed to die because we are *never* allowed to kill the innocent. Two deaths are better than one murder. Many find that sort of reasoning an affront to common sense. And more recently the Johns Hopkins case, allowing the baby to starve to death rather than mercifully terminating its life, has raised further doubts in the minds of many Catholics about the validity of the no direct killing principle. Even though they continue to hold it, growing numbers of them have a suspicion that there is something seriously wrong with it, but they don't know what or can't put it into words. That, I take it, was the reason the people I talked to refused to answer my question about the nurse in the Johns Hopkins-like case and chose instead to talk about the immorality of our cultural attitudes toward the elderly, the sick, the poor, and children in general. They had no doubts about what should be said in those cases and they easily found the words to convey their meaning.

What To Say About Killing

A lot of conceptual difficulties could have been avoided if our ancestors in faith had recorded the fifth commandment differently. By giving it the "Thou shalt not kill" form, they introduced an ambiguity into the matter which has haunted Jews and Christians ever since. If the commandment was meant to be absolute, then it should have been expressed by using a complete and determined moral term. Now "kill" is an incomplete and open moral term because it is always possible to ask whether the killing was "good" or "bad." But if from the moral point of view some killing is good and some bad, there cannot be an absolute prohibition against it. As we have now come to understand, the fifth commandment should have been given the form "Thou shalt do no murder" because "murder" is a complete and determinate moral term used to signify only the "bad" killings.[25] Our language, then, does not permit us to speak, from the moral point of view, either of an absolute prohibition against killing or of "good" murders. Only confusion awaits us when we proceed unmindful of that linguistic fact.

The issue then becomes one of determining what it is that renders some killings "good" and permissible and others "bad" and not morally permitted. Two things must be considered: Is the killing against the will of the one killed, and does it do her undeserved injury or harm? If so, the act is murder and is morally reprehensible. If not, then the act is an act of killing which is not morally wrong.[26] When, as St. Thomas More explains, a person is reduced to such a status that to kill her is no longer able to be interpreted as doing her harm, then the only thing preventing direct action is that person's consent. Since in cases of bona fide euthanasia both conditions are met, it is small wonder that reasonable people are for it.

What To Say About Killing vs. Letting Die

As has been shown, the issue of killing versus letting die is so complicated an issue that it has spawned an ever growing literature of its own. The Johns Hopkins case shows beyond doubt that we cannot simply say letting die is permissible and direct killing is not. "Letting die," like "killing," is an incomplete or open moral term and so there will be both a "good" and a "bad" instance of "letting die." Whether it is the one or the other can't be determined a priori but must be discerned in each instance from the circumstances of the case. It might be reasonable to assume that in cases where the conditions for permissible direct killing are not met, it is probably equally wrong to let the person die. But that too would have to be determined afresh in each case.

Other similarities between killing and letting die emerge if one looks at "letting die" not as non-agency but rather as delayed agency. The reason moral responsibility is so clear in cases of direct killing is that there is no significant time lapse in achieving the effect. In "letting die" cases the time lapse between the omission and the dying deceives us into thinking that they are not causally related. But as contemporary action-theory attests, omissions can generate a delayed positive act for which the omitter is morally responsible.[27] If that is so then in many cases there might be no morally significant difference between killing and letting die, and in those cases the same conditions for moral permissibility would have to be met in either case.

Conclusion

Thinking the unthinkable was traumatic enough, attempting to justify it is enough to blow one's mind, especially if one is a middle-aged Catholic. Nonetheless, I remain convinced that my having made that effort does not disqualify me from walking with the Lord and claiming to be both Christian and Catholic. My community may still have its doubts about that. So be it. I am confident that if we all remain faithful to the Lord's dream for the world as we face the life/death decisions that lie ahead of us, those experiences will inevitably move us toward consensus. Agreement is a function of experience. And contrary to popular opinion, agreement on moral matters is not only possible, it is inevitable. Moral relativism is a temporary state at best. The human race is in agreement about the immorality of lying, stealing, violence, murder, etc. That agreement is the fruit of communally funded experience. The day must inevitably come when we finally agree on euthanasia, one way or the other. In the meantime, we live in an in-between time of temporary disagreement.

The startling advances in medical technology have pre-cipitated new experiences which we have yet to fully assimilate. True, we are presently in confusion and disagreement on the "right to die" issue, but unanimity is on the way. We can no more prevent its coming than we can hold back the dawn. And I am betting that when it comes, our admiration of Thomas More will be all the greater.

Notes

1. Augustine, *The City of God,* II, 21.

2. Aquinas, *Summa Theologiae,* II-II, 64.

3. Soren Kierkegaard, *Fear and Trembling,* Princeton University Press, Princeton, N.J., 1968.

4. Richard Westley, *What A Modern Catholic Believes About The Right To Life,* Thomas More, Chicago, 1973. Cf. p. 63.

5. *Summa Theologiae* II-II, 64, 5, c.

6. *Summa Theologiae* II-II, 64, 5, ad 3.

7. W. M. Gaylin, "Sharing The Hardest Decision," pp. 33-38; and R. I. Peck, "When Should The Patient Be Allowed To Die," pp. 29-33, in *Hospital Physician,* July, 1972.

See Also: *New York Times,* Oct. 15, 1971:31 and Oct. 17, 1971:33.

8. James Rachels, "Euthanasia, Killing and Letting Die," in John Ladd (ed.), *Ethical Issues Relating To Life and Death,* Oxford University Press, N.Y., 1979, pp. 146-163.

9. Joseph M. Boyle, Jr., "On Killing and Letting Die" in *The New Scholasticism,* Vol. 51 (1977), pp. 433-452.

Arthur J. Dyck, "An Alternative To The Ethic of Euthanasia," in Robert F. Weir (ed.), *Ethical Issues In Death & Dying,* Columbia University Press, 1977, pp. 281-296.

10. Lacking as we do a "theology of failure," we Catholics have generally made a real botch of coping with birth control, divorce and remarriage, the defections from priesthood and religious life, the loss of our children to other denominations or religions, as well as of those who claim the right to die. We must learn to be gracious in the face of failure to achieve our highest ideals, if for no other reason than in that we are all alike. We all fail. We must rid ourselves of the notion that being gracious in the face of failure is to somehow give up on the ideal. In short, we need a theology of failure.

11. Paige Mitchell, *Act of Love,* Alfred A. Knopf, N.Y., 1976, pp. 272-4.

12. James Carse & Arlene Dallery, *Death and Society,* Harcourt, Brace, Jovanovich, N.Y., 1977, p. 88.

13. With respect to proposition (2), more than a beginning has already been made. In fact, the literature seems to be concerned almost exclusively with that problem. Proposition (1) receives less attention because it is seen as a religious proposition not so readily amenable to rational discussion. I believe that to justify proposition (B) is insufficient to move believers from the liberal to the radical view, because for Catholics proposition (2) is really only a derived consequence of proposition (1). To be successful, one must deal with the more fundamental proposition. I have, therefore, undertaken to undermine proposition (1) directly by attempting to justify proposition (A) from faith. Since few, if any, have attempted that, I see what I am doing in this section as a modest beginning.

14. Other Catholics of the fundamentalist view go even farther and say that euthanasia is irrational and not in accord with reason. One has only to read the arguments of the pro-euthanasia literature to realize how wrong that assessment is. The point is, of course, that euthanasia could well accord with reason and still not be right, a point which must necessarily escape those who equate the rational with the moral.

15. Joseph V. Sullivan, "The Immorality of Euthanasia," in Marvin Kohl (ed.), *Beneficent Euthanasia,* Prometheus Books, Buffalo, 1975, p. 14.

16. Westley, *op. cit.,* pp. 15-26.

17. *Summa Theologiae,* I-II, 100, 1, c.

18. *De Malo,* II, 4, c.

19. Robert Johann, *Building The Human,* Herder & Herder, N.Y. 1968, pp. 26-28.

20. Westley, *op. cit.,* pp. 73-81.

21. Bernard Gert, *The Moral Rules,* Harper Torchbook, N.Y., 1973, pp. 20-43.

22. St. Thomas More, *Utopia,* ed. Edward Surtz, S.J., Yale University Press, New Haven, 1964, pp. 108-109.

23. 1) On Whether killing is ever permissible, see:

Richard Brandt, "A Moral Principle About Killing," in Marvin Kohl, *Beneficent Euthanasia,* Prometheus, Buffalo, 1975, pp. 106-114.

Dan Brock, "Moral Rights and Permissible Killing," in John Ladd, *Ethical Issues Relating to Life and Death,* Oxford University Press, N.Y., 1979, pp. 94-117.

2) On affirming the moral significance of the distinction between killing and letting die, see:

Joseph M. Boyle, Jr., "On Killing and Letting Die," in *The New Scholasticism,* Vol. 51 (1977), pp. 433-452.

Arthur J. Dyck, "An Alternative To The Ethic of Euthanasia," in Robert F. Weir, *Ethical Issues In Death and Dying,* Columbia University Press, N.Y., 1977, pp. 281-296.

William E. May, "Euthanasia, Benemortasia and The Dying," in Jersild & Johnson, *Moral Issues and Christian Response,* Holt, Rinehart & Winston, 2nd ed., N.Y. 1976, pp. 399-408.

3) On denying the moral significance of the distinction between killing and letting die, see:

John Ladd, "Positive and Negative Euthanasia," in John Ladd, *Ethical Issues Relating To Life and Death,* Oxford University Press, N.Y., 1979, pp. 164-186.

James Rachels, "Euthanasia, Killing and Letting Die,"in John Ladd, *Ibid.,* pp. 146-163.

Judith Jarvis Thomson, "Killing, Letting Die and the Trolley Problem," in *The Monist,* Vol. 59, No. 2 (April 1976), pp. 204-217.

24. Alan Donagan, *The Theory of Morality,* University of Chicago Press, Chicago, 1977, pp. 72-79.

25. Julius Kovesi, *Moral Notions,* Humanities Press, N.Y., 1971, pp. 92-143.

26. See the Richard Brandt article cited in note #23 above.

27. John Ladd, "Positive and Negative Euthanasia," in John Ladd, *Ethical Issues Relating To Life and Death,* Oxford University Press, 1979, N.Y., pp. 175-179.

An Annotated Bibliography

ACTON, H. B., "Does The End Justify The Means?," in Marcus Singer, *Morals & Values,* Charles Scribner's, New York, 1977, pp. 172-183.

Shows that the principle that the end justifies the means is not really tenable by showing its false presuppositions.

BEAUCHAMP, Tom & PERLIN, Seymour, *Ethical Issues In Death and Dying,* Prentice Hall, Englewood Cliffs, New Jersey, 1978.

A collection of essays. Section 2 is on Suicide, and Section 4 is on Euthanasia. Contains the Yale Kamisar and Glanville Williams exchange, as well as Rachel's important piece on active and passive euthanasia.

*BOYLE, JR., Joseph M., "On Killing and Letting Die," in *The New Scholasticism,* Vol. 51 (1977), pp. 433-452.

A strong defense of the moral relevance of the distinction between letting die and killing against Rachels and Thomson. Contains a good evaluation of the Johns Hopkins case. Strangely enough no mention is made of the freedom or will of the patient.

*BRANDT, Richard, "A Moral Principle About Killing" in Marvin Kohl, *Beneficent Euthanasia,* Prometheus, Buffalo, 1975, pp. 106-114.

Excellent. In this short essay Brandt shows that the prohibition against killing is not a primary moral principle. He effectively shows that killing is morally evil only if it inflicts injury and is against the person's will.

BROCK, Dan, "Moral Rights and Permissible Killing," in John Ladd, *Ethical Issues Relating To Life and Death,* Oxford University Press, N.Y., 1979, pp. 94-117.

Argues that utilitarian cost/benefit reasoning is inadequate in determining if killing is morally permissible. The matter cannot be settled without a theory of distributive justice and human rights.

CARSE, James & DALLERY, Arlene, *Death and Society,* Harcourt, Brace, Jovanovich, N.Y., 1977.

A book of readings. Section II on Euthanasia is very good with articles by Flew, Rachels, Ramsey, Fletcher, et. al.

*DONAGAN, Alan, *The Theory of Morality,* University of Chicago Press, Chicago, 1977.

An excellent contemporary account of the role of reason in traditional Western morality. A masterful book of profound scholarship. A *must* for those into moral philosophy and theology.

DYCK, Arthur J., "An Alternative To The Ethic of Euthanasia," in Robert F. Weir *Ethical Issues In Death & Dying,* Columbia University Press, N.Y., 1977, pp. 281-296.

Invents the term "benemortasia" for a good death that does not include mercy killing as the "euthanasia" does. Goes on to contrast the ethics of benemortasia to the ethics of euthanasia.

*FOOT, Philippa, "Euthanasia," in John Ladd, *Ethical Issues Relating to Life and Death,* Oxford University Press, N.Y., 1979, pp. 14-40.

Excellent article. Shows that one can never call a killing "euthanasia" unless it is done not for the good of the survivors but rather for the good of the one killed.

GAYLIN, W. M., "Sharing The Hardest Decision" in *Hospital Physician,* July, 1972, pp. 33-38.

An account of the Johns Hopkins case.

*GERT, Bernard, *The Moral Rules,* Harper Torchbook, Harper Row, N.Y., 1973.

A *must* for the student of ethics. Presents a rational foundation for ethics, but in the process shows that reason gives morality support only within strict limits. Very good.

JOHANN, Robert O., *Freedom and Value,* Fordham University Press, N.Y., 1976.

A collection of nine essays by distinguished members of the Fordham University philosophy faculty. A bi-centennial book, its focus is on freedom and moral, social and political values.

*KAVANAUGH, Robert E., *Facing Death,* Penguin, 1974.

Superlative book. Must reading for anyone for whom the thought of death is terrifying. The section on coping with grief and its stages and therapy are matchless and should not be missed.

*KOHL, Marvin, *Beneficent Euthanasia,* Prometheus Books, Buffalo, 1975.

A truly fine collection of essays, edited with an open mind by a pro-euthanasia advocate. Especially important are the essays by Sullivan, Maguire, Fletcher, Dyck and Brandt.

—— *The Morality of Killing,* Peter Owens, London, 1974.

A pro-euthanasia advocate gives a reasoned account of his position. A short book of high quality.

KOVESI, Julius, *Moral Notions,* Humanities Press, 1971.

A remarkable book in meta-ethics. Especially good on the role of language in shaping moral discourse.

*LADD, John, *Ethical Issues Relating to Life and Death,* Oxford University Press, 1979.

Undoubtedly one of the finest collections of readings available. The two essays by the editor himself may well be the best of the lot. Must reading. Superior.

—— "The Definition of Death and The Right To Die," pp. 118-145 in the above.

Superior—an illuminating account of the practical importance of the definition of death followed by a brilliant account of the "right to die." Ladd questions speaking of "rights" in the life/death issues because virtue, love and concern seems to be called for.

—— "Positive and Negative Euthanasia," pp. 164-186 in the above.

A serious and powerful presentation which questions the moral relevance of the distinction between killing and letting die on the basis of the generation of an act-tree. The distinction fails to see that omissions generate positive acts. Warns proponents of the distinction against the fallacy of the simple description of acts. Excellent.

*MAGUIRE, Daniel C., *Death By Choice,* Schocken Books, N.Y., 1975.

A courageous book by a Catholic and *must* reading for anyone attempting to understand the rationale of the current shift among growing numbers of Catholic scholars on this question. Meticulously done, brilliantly conceived, and yet eminently readable by the general public. A gold mine. Absolutely indispensable to any Catholic wanting to get into this problem.

——"A Catholic View of Mercy Killing" in Marvin Kohl, *Beneficent Euthanasia,* Prometheus, Buffalo, 1975, pp. 34-43.

A short article showing the possibility of more than one Catholic position on mercy killing. Tame and reserved in the light of his brilliant *Death By Choice* book.

MAY, William E., "Euthanasia, Benemortasia and The Dying" in Jersild & Johnson, *Moral Issues & Christian Response,* Holt, Rinehart & Winston, 2nd ed., N.Y., 1976, pp. 399-408.

An account of the ethics of benemortasia vs. the ethics of euthanasia. Interesting treatment of the truck driver case, as the author pushes the traditional position to its limits.

MITCHELL, Paige, *Act of Love,* Alfred A. Knopf, N.Y., 1976.

A disturbing book. An account of how Lester Zygmaniak shot and killed his brother George at the latter's request after an accident that left him a quadraplegic. Mitchell's account of the subsequent trial and the thought processes of the defense attorney and of the author himself is impressive. Excellent for those interested in the legal aspects of Euthanasia.

PECK, R. I., "When Should The Patient Be Allowed To Die," in Hospital Physician, July, 1972, pp. 29-33. More on the Johns Hopkins Case.

*RACHELS, James, "Euthanasia, Killing and Letting Die" in John Ladd, *Ethical Issues Relating to Life and Death,* Oxford University Press, N.Y., 1979, pp. 146-163.

Important. A powerful attack on the moral relevance of the distinction between killing and letting die in the light of Johns Hopkins type cases. Attempts to show that letting die can be less good and merciful than killing. The case Rachels makes has become an integral part of the current debate.

*RUSSELL, O. Ruth, *Freedom To Die,* Human Sciences Press, New York, Revised ed., 1977.

An excellent source book of facts and historical information on the Euthanasia question. Outlines the various arguments pro and con. A good place to begin study of the problem even though the author is pro-euthanasia.

*STODDARD, Sandol, *The Hospice Movement,* Vintage Book, Random House, N.Y., 1978.

A lucid account of the Hospice Movement, its history and philosophy. Highlights how truly inadequate and scandalous our present system of caring for the terminally ill is. An inspiring book.

SULLIVAN, Joseph V., "The Immorality of Euthanasia," in Marvin Kohl, *Beneficent Euthanasia,* Prometheus Books, Buffalo, 1975, pp. 12-33.

An anti-euthanasia account of traditional Catholic position by moral theologian Sullivan, who is now a bishop.

THOMSON, Judith Jarvis, "Killing, Letting Die, and The Trolley Problem" in *The Monist,* Vol. 59, No. 2, (April 1976), pp. 204-217.

A serious, well reasoned but humorous account of the killing vs. letting die problem. Shows how philosophers can knit-pick and still enjoy their work.

*WALSH, Michael, MOFFAT, Ronald, CORBISHLY, Thomas, et. al., *The Quality of Death,* Templegate, Springfield, Ill., 1975.

Done in England at the height of the euthanasia debates there, this book is a collection of articles covering many facets of the problem. Centers on the sort of care the terminally ill require and have a right to. Hospices receive attention in this presentation.

WEIR, Robert F., *Ethical Issues in Death and Dying,* Columbia University Press, N.Y., 1977.

An excellent anthology of articles. Section 3 has to do with allowing to die. Section 4 with euthanasia. Notable contributors are: Gustafson, McCormick, Ramsey, Fletcher, Dyck, et. al.

WESTLEY, Richard, *What A Modern Catholic Believes About The Right To Life,* Thomas More, Chicago, 1973.

*WILSON, Jerry B., *Death By Decision,* Westminster Press, Philadelphia, 1975.

Excellent. A small but most comprehensive book, as its sub-title attests: *The Medical, Moral and Legal Dilemmas of Euthanasia.* The book though small lives up to its sub-title and then some. It is a remarkable piece of work. Wilson's ability to get at the essentials of the positions of others make this book a treasure. See especially Chp. 3 on Conflicting Religious Views. An excellent place to begin study.